# Ancient History

## Recent Work and
## New Directions

**Publications of the**
## Association of Ancient Historians

The purpose of the monograph series is to survey the state of the current scholarship in various areas of ancient history.

#1  Past and Future in Ancient History
   *Chester G. Starr*

#2  The Shifting Sands of History: Interpretations of
      Ptolemaic Egypt
   *Alan E. Samuel*

#3  Roman Imperial Grand Strategy
   *Arther Ferrill*

#4  Myth Becomes History: Pre-Classical Greece
   *Carol G. Thomas*

**Other publications by the Association**

Makedonika: Essays by Eugene N. Borza
   *Edited by Carol G. Thomas*

# Ancient History:
## Recent Work and New Directions

Publications of the
Association of
Ancient Historians 5

**Stanley M. Burstein**
**Ramsay MacMullen**
**Kurt A. Raaflaub**
**Allen M. Ward**
*Directed by*
**Carol G. Thomas**

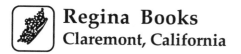 **Regina Books**
Claremont, California

10   9   8   7   6   5   4   3   2   1

**Library of Congress Cataloging-in-Publication Data**

Ancient history : recent work and new directions / Stanley M. Burstein . . . [et al.] ; directed by Carol G. Thomas.
       p.       cm. -- (Publications of the Association of Ancient Historians ; 5)
       Includes bibliographical references.
       ISBN 0-941690-79-2 (cloth : alk. paper). -- ISBN 0-941690-78-4 (pap : alk. paper)
       1. Greece--History--To 145 B.C.--Historiography. 2. Greece--History--146 B.C.-323 A.D..--Historiography. 3. Rome--Historiography. I. Burstein, Stanley Mayer. II. Thomas, Carol G., 1938-  . III. Series
DE8.A54 1997
938--dc21                                     97-35440
                                           CIP

Co-published by arrangement with the
Association of Ancient Historians

𝕽𝖊𝖌𝖎𝖓𝖆 𝕭𝖔𝖔𝖐𝖘
Post Office Box 280
Claremont, California 91711
Tel: (909) 624-8466 / Fax (909) 626-1345

Manufactured in the United States of America.

# CONTENTS

# ABBREVIATIONS

| | |
|---|---|
| A&A | Antike und Abendland |
| AC | Acta Classica |
| AHR | American Historical Review |
| AJA | American Journal of Archaeology |
| AJAH | American Journal of Ancient History |
| ANRW | Aufstieg und Niedergang der römischen Welt (1972-) |
| AncSoc | Ancient Society |
| APA | American Philological Association |
| BAR | British Archaeological Reports |
| BCH | Bulletin de correspondance hellénique |
| Bryn Mawr Class Rev | Bryn Mawr Classical Review |
| BSA | The Annual of the British School at Athens |
| CA | Classical Antiquity |
| CJ | Classical Journal |
| CP | Classical Philology |
| CQ | Classical Quarterly |
| CW | Classical World |
| DHA | Dialogues d'Histoire Ancienne |
| G&R | Greece and Rome |
| Hist Sci | History of Science |
| HSCP | Harvard Studies in Classical Philology |
| HZ | Historische Zeitschrift |
| ICS | Illinois Classical Studies |
| IJCT | International Journal of the Classical Tradition |
| ILS | Inscriptiones Latinae Selectae |

| | |
|---|---|
| JHS | Journal of Hellenic Studies |
| JMA | Journal of Mediterranean Archaeology |
| JRA | Journal of Roman Archaeology |
| JRS | Journal of Roman Studies |
| JTS | Journal of Theological Studies |
| MH | Museum Helveticum |
| OCD | Oxford Classical Dictionary |
| P&P | Past and Present |
| PCPhS | Proceedings of the Cambridge Philological Society |
| RM | Römische Mitteilungen |
| SEG | Supplementum Epigraphicum Graecum |
| SO | Symbolae osloenses |
| WS | Wiener Studien |
| ZPE | Zeitschrift für Papyrologie und Epigraphik |

## PREFACE

The inaugural volume of the *Publications of the Association of Ancient Historians* provided an overview of recent trends and possible future areas of investigation in Greek and Roman studies extending from late Dark Age Greece through the collapse of the Roman Empire in the west. Chester Starr, first president of the Association, accepted this challenge, perhaps rather less daunting to him than it would have been to most by reason of his vast knowledge of the whole of the ancient Mediterranean world. Published in 1987 by University Press of America, the volume quickly accomplished its purpose of furthering teaching and study of ancient history. In addition to its distribution to all current members of the Association it was sold by the publisher—in fact, it was sold-out and not reprinted.

Three subsequent publications have appeared and several more have been commissioned, all examining recent trends in scholarship albeit in more limited aspects of antiquity. As the list of more specialized titles grew, it seemed important to provide a current overview of the broad sweep of ancient Greek and Roman studies; our study of the deep past DOES change even in the space of a single decade.

Basic divisions of the subject have not changed, however, so the current review uses the model of the earlier volume: sections treat, in turn, Greece, the Hellenistic Age including Macedon, the Roman Republic, and the Roman Empire. Areas of both continuity and change over the last ten years are tracked. Each section has been compiled by a specialist in that aspect of ancient history, though each of the four—time and other commitments permitting—could have produced the entire volume, such is the scholarly accomplishment of each contributor. A second criterion was key in the search for compilers, namely dedication to the work of our Association. In fact, this factor proved to be a useful persuasive device in more than one case!

In order of their discussions, you will find Kurt Raaflaub's *Greece*; Stanley Burstein, *The Hellenistic Age*; Allen Ward on *The Roman Republic*, and Ramsay MacMullen's treatment of *The Roman Empire*. A concise, general bibliography occurs in a final section. Brief notes on the contributors are found at the end of this volume.

While following Starr's model, each scholar's discussion is idiosyncratic, "reflecting the author's own interests and knowledge," in the words of Kurt Raaflaub. Yet the audience in view remains similar to that envisioned by Starr. As Ramsay MacMullen put the matter well in an oral version of his contribution, "I imagined myself addressing the same audience that I think [Starr] had in mind…an ancient historian, beginning or advanced, who is addressing some particular corner of it—maybe someone who's most familiar with the Bronze Age but now wants some quick update on the centuries A.D.: what's new in that area?"

The frequent appearance of Chester Starr's name in these few pages indicates far more than use of his volume as a model: he is held in the highest esteem and affection as a teacher, colleague, scholar, and friend by countless numbers of people. And so we dedicate this effort to him, in the spirit of words he once offered to his mentor, M. L. W. Laistner (quoted in A. Ferrill and T. Kelly, edd., *Chester G. Starr. Essays on Ancient History* [Leiden 1979] xii):

Te sequor…inque tuis nunc
Ficta pedum pono pressis vestigia signis.

Carol Thomas

# I

## GREECE

*Kurt A. Raaflaub*

Chester Starr gave us a hard act to follow.[1] Surveys of recent scholarship are inevitably idiosyncratic, reflecting the authors' own interests and knowledge—and especially the gaps in their knowledge. Given the limited space available, even coverage of all periods and areas is impossible; hence I shall deliberately focus on one period, the archaic (which perhaps is less familiar to most and where recent developments seem especially exciting), and touch only briefly on the fifth and fourth centuries, and I shall omit almost completely the history of political and military events.

My approach differs from Starr's in two ways. He declared, "This is not a bibliographical essay" (ix). I would like to offer both a (selective) bibliographical essay and a critical evaluation, highlighting developments and debates and pointing out shortcomings. Starr also gave preference, "as far as possible," "to books and journals in English or translated." I shall cast my net more widely: much important work that cannot be ignored here has been published in languages other than English.

### I

The year 1987 witnessed the publication not only of Starr's booklet but also of Martin Bernal's *Black Athena*. The debate about this work has become a fierce and often frustrating clash of cultural expectations and ideologies. Despite many good observations, Bernal's thesis seems vastly exaggerated, his

---

[1] C. Starr, *Past and Future in Ancient History* (Lanham MD 1987), cited by name only. All dates are BCE. I thank Carla Antonaccio, Andrea Berlin, Deborah Boedeker, Paul Cartledge, Charles Hamilton, Askold Ivantchik, Paul Keyser, John Kroll, Rob Loomis, Deborah Lyons, Catherine Morgan, Ian Morris, Brian Rose, Carol Thomas and Larry Tritle for helpful suggestions.

methodology significantly flawed, his results, as claimed, often unacceptable. Cultural relations between the ancient Near East and the Hellenic world were rich and complex; the Greeks did not simply import or "steal" their culture from others.[2] But Bernal deserves credit for raising general awareness that contacts with other cultures, near and far, in both the second and first millennia, were a crucial component of Greek cultural development and that Greek history cannot be treated in isolation. Hence here, too, these aspects must not be missing.

A number of recent works have made it easier for Hellenists to inform themselves about Near Eastern and Egyptian history.[3] Similarly, an increasing number of detailed studies have focused on Near Eastern (Mesopotamian, Hittite, Phoenician) and Egyptian influences on various aspects of Greek thought and literature (myths, epics, theogonies, cosmogonies, wisdom literature), the beginnings of Greek science (especially mathematics and astronomy), political reflection and philosophy, the development of Greek religion, crafts, art and architecture, technology (both civil and military), coinage, and writing, and, although these aspects are more debated, social, legal, and political phenomena, such as tyranny, the enactment of written law, the symposium, and perhaps the polis.[4] We now know more about the presence of Greeks in the

---

[2] M. Bernal, *Black Athena: the Afroasiatic Roots of Classical Civilization*, 2 vols. (New Brunswick NJ 1987, 1991); see *The Challenge of "Black Athena," Arethusa*, special issue 1989; M. Lefkowitz and G. Rogers (edd), *Black Athena Revisited* (Chapel Hill 1996); M. Lefkowitz, *Not Out of Africa: How Afrocentrism Became an Excuse to Teach Myth as History* (New York 1996); S. Burstein, "The Debate about Black Athena," *Scholia* 5 (1996) 3-16.

[3] Apart from the early volumes of the new edition of the *Cambridge Ancient History* (by now already somewhat outdated), see J. Sasson (ed), *Civilizations of the Ancient Near East*, 4 vols. (New York 1995); A. Kuhrt, *The Ancient Near East, c. 3000-330 B.C.*, 2 vols. (London 1995); J. Assmann, *Ma'at: Gerechtigkeit und Unsterblichkeit im Alten Ägypten* (Munich 1990); P. Briant, *Histoire de l'empire Perse de Cyrus à Alexandre* (Paris 1996); cf. also H. Saggs, *Civilization before Greece and Rome* (New Haven 1989); V. Krings (ed), *La civilisation phénicienne et punique: Manuel de recherche* (Leiden 1995).

[4] J. Bouzek, *Greece, Anatolia and Europe: Interrelations during the Early Iron Age* (Stockholm 1997; cf. id., *The Aegean, Anatolia and Europe: Cultural Interrelations in the Second Millennium BC* [Prague 1985]); cf. P. Haider, *Griechenland-Nordafrika: Ihre Beziehungen zwischen 1500 und 600 v. Chr.* (Darmstadt 1988); W. Burkert, *The Orientalizing Revolution* (Cambridge MA 1992); id., "Homerstudien und Orient," in J. Latacz (ed), *Zweihundert Jahre Homer-Forschung* (Stuttgart 1991) 155-81; G. Kopcke and I. Tokumaru (edd), *Greece*

Levant and Egypt, while the presence of Phoenicians in the Aegean (especially on Crete) is established beyond doubt.[5] What seems needed now is a comprehensive re-evaluation of the significance of such influences on Greek social and cultural developments, of the ways in which the Greeks absorbed and transformed such influences, and of the impulses they gave to developments in the countries with which they communicated. Although influences may have been stronger in one direction than in the other, it might be helpful to look at this process as one of interaction, and the suggestion is worth pursuing that we should perhaps think of an intellectual and cultural *koinē* in the eastern Mediterranean during various periods of the second and first millennia.[6] In comparison to the south and east—and, for that matter, the west—Greek interaction with the Celtic north remains less thoroughly explored.[7]

Heleen Sancisi-Weerdenburg has long insisted that too often Persian society, customs, and politics are interpreted solely on the basis of Greek reports on Persia. "It is generally recognised

*between East and West: 10th to 8th Centuries B.C.* (Mainz 1992); S. Burstein, "Greek Contact with Egypt and the Levant: ca. 1600-500 B.C.," *Ancient World* 27 (1996) 20-28. For studies of individual aspects, see the bibliography cited in K. Raaflaub and E. Müller-Luckner (edd), *Anfänge politischen Denkens in der Antike. Die nahöstlichen Kulturen und die Griechen* (Munich 1993) xviii n.40, to which should be added the chapters in the same vol. by H. Matthäus on art and culture (165-86) and V. Fadinger on tyranny (263-316); S. Morris, *Daidalos and the Origins of Greek Art* (Princeton 1992); "Homer and the Near East," in B. Powell and I. Morris (edd), *A New Companion to Homer* (Leiden 1997) 599-623; C. Ulf (ed), *Wege zur Genese griechischer Identität* (Berlin 1996), and a forthcoming book by M. West. See generally, S. Humphreys, "Diffusion, Comparison, Criticism," in Raaflaub and Müller-Luckner, 1-11.

[5] In addition to titles cited in n.4, see T. Braun, in *CAH* III.3² (1982) 1-56; W. Gehrig and H. Niemeyer (edd), *Die Phönizier im Zeitalter Homers* (Mainz 1990); M. Aubet, *The Phoenicians and the West* (Cambridge 1993); P. Haider, "Griechen im Vorderen Orient und in Ägypten bis ca. 590 v.Chr.," in Ulf (n.4) 59-115; A. Möller, *Naucratis as Port of Trade* (Oxford, forthcoming); G. Hoffman, *Imports and Immigrants: Near Eastern Contacts with Iron Age Crete* (Ann Arbor MI, forthcoming).

[6] K. Seybold and J. von Ungern-Sternberg, "Amos und Hesiod. Aspekte eines Vergleichs," in Raaflaub and Müller-Luckner (n.4) 215-39.

[7] Bouzek (n.4); D. Harding, "Celtic Europe," *CAH* VI² (1994) 404-21; K. Arafat and C. Morgan, "Athens, Etruria and the Heuneburg: Mutual Misconceptions in the Study of Greek-Barbarian Relations," in I. Morris (ed), *Classical Greece: Ancient Histories and Modern Archaeologies* (Cambridge 1994) 108-34. Black Sea area and western Mediterranean: n.10.

that these Greek sources are biased and present Persian matters with a definite slant...But having said this, the usual procedure is to follow these very same Greek sources, usually while ignoring evidence from Persia or discarding it as basically unreliable. In matters regarding the Persian empire we are still very much under the tyranny of Greece." In a series of "Achaemenid History Workshops" Sancisi-Weerdenburg and her colleagues have done much to correct and improve the picture.[8] Classicists, too, have examined relations between Greeks and especially the Persian Empire, and the impact their confrontation with this mighty neighbor had on Greek thinking and behavior.[9] Relations between Greeks and non-Greeks have been studied in other areas as well, including Greek perceptions of the northern nomad peoples (Scythians, Kimmerians, and Iranian tribes) and relations with native peoples in "colonial" areas. In the Black Sea region, the fall of the Iron Curtain has facilitated collaboration between western and eastern scholars, with very positive results.[10]

---

[8] H. Sancisi-Weerdenburg, "Political Concepts in Old-Persian Royal Inscriptions," in Raaflaub and Müller-Luckner (n.4) 145-63 (cit. 145-46); ead. *et al.* (edd), *Achaemenid History* I-VIII (Leiden 1987-1994); cf. Briant (n.3).

[9] E. Hall, *Inventing the Barbarian: Greek Self-Definition through Tragedy* (Oxford 1989); "Asia Unmanned: Images of Victory in Classical Athens," in J. Rich and G. Shipley (edd), *War and Society in the Greek World* (London 1993) 108-33; P. Georges, *Barbarian Asia and the Greek Experience* (Baltimore 1994); L. Steel, "Challenging Preconceptions of Oriental 'Barbarity' and Greek 'Humanity': Human Sacrifice in the Ancient World," in N. Spencer (ed), *Time, Tradition and Society in Greek Archaeology: Bridging the Great Divide* (London 1995) 18-27; M. Miller, *Athens and Persia in the Fifth Century B.C.: A Study in Cultural Receptivity* (Cambridge 1997).

[10] Generally: *Modes de contacts et processus de transformation dans les sociétés anciennes* (Pisa and Rome 1983); J.-P. Descoeudres (ed), *Greek Colonists and Native Populations* (Canberra and Oxford 1990); P. Cartledge, *The Greeks* (Oxford 1993), ch. 3; A. Dihle, *Die Griechen und die Fremden* (Munich 1994); G. Tsetskhladze and F. De Angelis (edd), *The Archaeology of Greek Colonisation* (Oxford 1994); cf. *Hérodote et les peuples non Grecs* (Vandoeuvres 1990). Nomads: A. Ivantchik, *Die eurasischen Nomaden im 8.-7. Jh. v. Chr. Griechische Literaturtradition und archäologische Zeugnisse* (Berlin, forthcoming); cf. id., *Les Cimmériens au Proche-Orient* (Fribourg and Göttingen 1993). West: C. Ampolo and T. Caruso, "I Greci e gli altri nel Mediterraneo occidentale," *Opus* 9-10 (1990-91) 29-58; P. Rouillard, *Les Grecs et la péninsule Ibérique du VIII<sup>e</sup> au IV<sup>e</sup> s. av. J.-C.* (Paris 1991); D. Ridgway, *The First Western Greeks* (Cambridge 1992); K. Lomas, "The Greeks in the West and the Hellenization of Italy," in Powell (n.35) 347-67; *Les Grecs et l'occident* (Rome 1995); H. Niemeyer, *Interactions in the Iron Age: Phoenicians, Greeks and*

## II

Before I move on, I should mention some recent handbooks and surveys. Apart from the new edition of the *Cambridge Ancient History*, the multi-authored *I Greci* offers a wide range of stimulating essays with good bibliographies.[11] Among single-authored surveys, those by Oswyn Murray and Robin Osborne on early Greece deserve highest praise.[12] So, incidentally, does the new *Oxford Classical Dictionary*: with many new entries that are of interest to the historian, it is much better than its detractors claim. The German *Der Neue Pauly*, fitting in between the monumental but largely outdated Pauly-Wissowa and the all too brief *Der Kleine Pauly*, promises to become a useful tool for information and research.[13]

Returning to history, for the Bronze and early Iron Ages we now have Carol Thomas' elegant and informative survey.[14] The problem of the end of the Bronze Age civilizations continues to be discussed intensely.[15] So does that of the nature of the early Iron Age. Traditionally called the "Dark Ages," this period

---

*the Indigenous Peoples of the Western Mediterranean* (Mainz 1996); R. Leighton, *Early Societies in Sicily: New Developments in Archaeological Research* (London 1996). Black Sea: G. Tsetskhladze, "Colchians, Greeks and Achaemenids in the 7th-5th Centuries BC," *Klio* 76 (1994) 78-102; id., in *I Greci* II.1 (n.11) 945-73; id. (ed), *The Greek Colonisation of the Black Sea* (forthcoming); K. Marchenko and J. Vinogradov, *The Greeks and Native Populations in the North Black Sea Region* (forthcoming). 4th century: N. Hammond, Z. Archibald, J. Hind, in *CAH* VI² (1994).

[11] S. Settis (ed), *I Greci: Storia, cultura, arte, società* (Turin 1995ff.; so far I and II.1); cf. M. Grant and R. Kitzinger (edd), *Civilizations of the Ancient Mediterranean*, 3 vols. (New York 1988); J. Boardman *et al.* (edd), *The Oxford History of the Classical World* I: *Greece and the Hellenistic World* (Oxford 1988).

[12] O. Murray, *Early Greece* (Cambridge MA ²1993); R. Osborne, *Greece in the Making, 1200-479 B.C.* (London 1996). 5th cent.: n.72; 4th cent.: n.111.

[13] S. Hornblower and A. Spawforth (edd), *The Oxford Classical Dictionary* (Oxford ³1996); H. Cancik and H. Schneider (edd), *Der Neue Pauly: Enzyklopädie der Antike* (Stuttgart 1996ff.; so far I).

[14] C. Thomas, *Myth Becomes History: Pre-Classical Greece* (Claremont CA 1993); cf. O. Dickinson, *The Aegean Bronze Age* (Cambridge 1994); J. Bennet, "Homer and the Bronze Age," in Powell and Morris (n.4) 511-34; P. Rehak (ed), *The Role of the Ruler in the Prehistoric Aegean*, 2 vols. (Brussels and Austin TX 1995); R. Laffineur and W.-D. Niemeier (edd), *Politeia: Society and State in the Aegean Bronze Age* (ibid. 1995).

[15] Briefly, Thomas (n.14) 66-67; cf. D. Musti *et al.* (edd), *La transizione dal miceneo all'alto arcaismo* (Rome 1991); W. Ward and M. Joukowsky (edd), *The Crisis Years: The 12th Century B.C.* (Dubuque IA 1992); R. Drews, *The End of the Bronze Age* (Princeton 1993).

(roughly 1200-800) has been illuminated by archaeological exploration. How should we interpret the changes reflected throughout this period? Opinions diverge widely. Long ago, Finley insisted that a deep gap separated the Bronze and Archaic Ages and assumed a break at the end of the former. Emily Vermeule countered, "There was no break between the Mycenaean and Homeric worlds, only change. The degree of change is arguable."[16] Certainly, as Starr observed already (2-3), the immense significance of this period in shaping the culture of later centuries is now increasingly recognized, and the concept of a "Dark Age," with relatively sharp chronological boundaries, has itself been challenged. In some outlying areas (Cyprus, Crete, to a lesser degree Athens or northern Boeotia/Phokis, among others) continuity was broad and substantial, and we now know that not all components of Mycenaean civilization were wiped out immediately. Rather than sweeping generalizations, we need to differentiate carefully between regions and issues or objects, and new discoveries are likely to cause further reassessments. Opinions still clash, on the overall nature of the period as well as on partial questions such as how far the depopulation and isolation of the Greek world in the "darkest period" really went or how exceptional or typical Lefkandi was.[17] At this point, the destruction of the palaces, the

---

[16] M. Finley, *Economy and Society in Ancient Greece* (New York 1982) 213, 232; see now Bennett (n.14). E. Vermeule, *Greece in the Bronze Age* (Chicago 1964) 309; cf. S. Morris, "Introduction," in Kopcke and Tokumaru (n.4) xiii-xviii; Thomas, *Myth* (n.14) 69; J. Latacz, "Between Troy and Homer," in *Storia, poesia e pensiero nel mondo antico: Studi...Marcello Gigante* (Naples 1994) 347-63; L. Foxhall, "Bronze to Iron: Agricultural Systems and Political Structures in Late Bronze Age and Early Iron Age Greece," *BSA* 90 (1995) 239-50. On the following, see Raaflaub, "A Historian's Headache: How to Read 'Homeric Society'?" in N. Fisher and H. van Wees (edd), *Archaic Greece: New Evidence and New Approaches* (Cardiff and London, forthcoming), with more bibliography.

[17] B. Patzek, *Homer und Mykene* (Munich 1992), pt. 2; Thomas (n.14) 69-82; I. Morris, "Homer and the Iron Age," in Morris and Powell (n.4) 535-59. On the debate about the "Dark Ages," see also J. Papadopoulos, "'Dark Age' Greece," forthcoming in *Oxford Companion for Archaeology*, and the debate between id. and I. Morris in *JMA* 6 (1993) 175-221; cf. Morris, "Periodization and the Heroes: Inventing a Dark Age," in M. Golden and P. Toohey (edd), *Inventing Classical Culture?* (London 1996) 96-131. Lefkandi: M. Popham *et al.*, *Lefkandi*, 2 vols. (London 1980, 1993); I. Morris, in Powell and Morris, 543-44, emphasizes exceptionality. S. Deger-Jalkotzy, "Elateia (Phokis) und die frühe Geschichte der Griechen," *Anzeiger der Österreichischen Akad. der Wiss.* 127 (1990) 77-86; "Die Erforschung des

nerve centers of Mycenaean economy and society, still appears as a traumatic event with irreversible consequences. The general impression of the "Submycenaean period" (ca. 1125-1050) still is one of a massively reduced population living in small and scattered villages, in simple conditions and in relative isolation. To cite Ian Morris, "If any period can truly be called a 'Dark Age,' it is this."[18] The Protogeometric and Geometric periods represent many new beginnings, and especially the eighth century witnessed rapid changes, a veritable "structural revolution," in which, as Morris says, "everything was open to challenge: the world was turned upside down."[19] Hence, even if the headings of "continuity" and "discontinuity," under which this debate has often been waged, are too broad and misleading, even if, as Thomas suggests, the component of violent rupture was relatively small and that of ongoing transformation large, such transformation was deep and comprehensive. The archaic world was indeed radically different from that of the Bronze Age four hundred years earlier.

## III

This brings us to the Archaic period, the focus of this survey.[20] Starr's remark, "No study of Greek history written more than two decades ago is now adequate for the period before 500" (3), is equally valid today. I group my observations around the rise of the polis. For its earliest history, archaeology and the Homeric epics are the main sources. In the 1970s the archaeological aspects received much attention, culminating in the masterful surveys of Snodgrass and Coldstream; by now, however, these no longer reflect the state of our knowledge. A new comprehensive archaeological survey is an urgent desideratum; Ian Morris' recent articles represent first steps in

---

Zusammenbruchs der sogenannten mykenischen Kultur und der sogenannten dunklen Jahrhunderte," in Latacz (n.4) 127-54, stresses continuity.

[18] In Morris and Powell (n.4) 540-41; cf. A. Snodgrass, *An Archaeology of Greece* (Berkeley 1987), ch.6; W. Donlan, "The Pre-State Community in Greece," *SO* 64 (1989) 5-29. J. Muhly, "The Crisis Years in the Mediterranean World," in Ward and Joukowsky (n.15) 10-26, esp. 19-21, is more optimistic.

[19] I. Morris, "Archaeology and Archaic Greek History," forthcoming in Fisher and van Wees (n.16); cf. Patzek (n.17), 104-20; S. Langdon (ed), *New Light on a Dark Age: Exploring the Culture of Geometric Greece* (Columbia MO 1997). "Structural revolution": A. Snodgrass, *Archaic Greece: The Age of Experiment* (Berkeley 1980), chs.1-2.

[20] Snodgrass (n.19) remains essential; on the archaeological record and its relation to history, see now Morris (n.19); excellent surveys in Murray, Osborne (n.12).

that direction.[21] The same need exists for the question of Homer's usefulness as a historical source. Two recent compendia offer good introductions to many areas of Homeric studies.[22] Finley's *The World of Odysseus* is still indispensable but partly outdated. Finley argued that the Homeric description of the social background to the heroic events and actions is sufficiently consistent to allow us to recognize a society that makes sense from an anthropological perspective and can be fitted into a scheme of social evolution among early societies. Critics continue to be unpersuaded, claiming that Homeric society is essentially unhistorical because its description either reveals contradictions that seem unsurmountable, or represents a fiction or a hopeless mixture of elements from various stages of social development, ranging from the Mycenaean to the Archaic ages.[23] Yet several scholars examining social values as well as social and economic structures and relations have observed a high degree of consistency in Homer's social picture. Various studies of warfare and modes of fighting, the working and significance of political institutions, the conduct of interstate relations, or the customs of feasting have yielded further confirmation. Also recently, a number of scholars have broadly re-examined Homeric society and reached the same conclusion.[24] Informed reading of the text, careful attention to details, and judicious use of anthropological and sociological methods continue to help clarify the historical picture, for

---

[21] A. Snodgrass, *The Dark Age of Greece* (Edinburgh 1971); *Archaeology and the Rise of the Greek State* (Cambridge 1977); J. N. Coldstream, *Geometric Greece* (London 1977); *The Formation of the Greek Polis: Aristotle and Archaeology* (Opladen, 1984). Morris (nn.17, 19). See also Snodgrass, "Archaeology and the Study of the Greek City," in J. Rich and A. Wallace-Hadrill, *City and Country in the Ancient World* (London 1991) 1-23; "The Rise of the Polis: the Archaeological Evidence," in M. Hansen (ed), *The Ancient Greek City-State* (Copenhagen 1993) 30-40; earlier bibliography in Raaflaub, "Homer und die Geschichte des 8. Jh.s v. Chr.," in Latacz (n.4) 205-56, at 240-41.

[22] Latacz (n.4); Morris and Powell (n.4).

[23] M. Finley, *The World of Odysseus* (London ²1977). *Contra*, recently, Cartledge, in *I Greci* (n.11) II.1, 687-88. For fuller discussion, see Osborne (n.12), ch.5.

[24] C. Ulf, *Die homerische Gesellschaft* (Munich 1990); H. van Wees, *Status Warriors* (Amsterdam 1992); Patzek (n.17); cf., e.g., A. Adkins, "Homeric Ethics," in Morris and Powell (n.4) 694-713; W. Donlan, "The Homeric Economy," ibid. 649-67 (cf. next note); G. Herman, *Ritualised Friendship and the Greek City* (Cambridge 1987); Murray (n.12), ch.3; R. Seaford, *Reciprocity and Ritual* (Oxford 1994). For fuller discussion of the controversy, see Raaflaub (n.16); id., "Homeric Society," in Morris and Powell, 624-48.

example, concerning economic transactions such as gift- and other exchanges, or consensus-building in various forms of assemblies.[25]

The relation of the archaeological to the epic evidence remains controversial. Morris concludes that "the material world described by Homer cannot be paralleled by the excavated record from any single region of Greece at any single point within the Iron Age" and "that there is no way to use Iron Age archaeology to fix Homer in time or space." By contrast, Jan Paul Crielaard finds "that the new phenomena, which are manifest in the archaeological record of the eighth century and which together constitute the so-called Greek 'Renaissance,' are without exception attested in the epics"; he considers the depiction of the "world of Homer" both internally consistent and largely compatible with the archaeological evidence for the poet's time.[26]

If we essentially accept the historicity of Homeric society, its date becomes important. For reasons which have been largely discredited, Finley thought of the tenth and ninth century; recent scholarship has emphasized the poet's own time in the second half of the eighth or even the first half of the seventh century.[27] However that may be, continuity increasingly emerges between customs and institutions of Homeric society and those independently attested for archaic Greece from the seventh century. This concerns, for example, the role of *xenia*, elite connections across communal boundaries, and the conduct of foreign relations,[28] the processes of communal decision-

---

[25] W. Donlan, "Homeric *temenos* and the Land Economy of the Dark Age," *MH* 46 (1989) 129-45; "The Unequal Exchange between Glaucus and Diomedes in Light of the Homeric Gift-Economy," *Phoenix* 43 (1989) 1-15; "Duelling with Gifts in the *Iliad*: As the Audience Saw It," *Colby Quarterly* 29.3 (1993) 155-72; S. van Reden, *Exchange in Ancient Greece* (London 1995), pt. I; E. Flaig, "Das Konsensprinzip im homerischen Olymp," *Hermes* 122 (1994) 13-31; id., *Annales* HSS 52 (1997) 3-29.

[26] I. Morris (n.17) 539; J. P. Crielaard, "Homer, History and Archaeology," in id. (ed), *Homeric Questions* (Amsterdam 1995) 201-88, at 273-75, cf. 201-9.

[27] Finley (n.23) 47-48; *contra*: I. Morris, "The Use and Abuse of Homer," *CA* 5 (1986) 81-138. 8th century: G. Kirk, *The Iliad: A Commentary* I (Cambridge 1985) 1-10; J. Latacz, *Homer: His Art and His World* (Ann Arbor 1996) 56-65. 7th cent.: Crielaard (n.26); M. West, "The Date of the Iliad," *MH* 52 (1995) 203-19; more bibliography in Raaflaub (n.16) n.77.

[28] Herman (n.24); E. Baltrusch, *Symmachie und Spondai* (Berlin 1994; for a different perspective, P. Karavites, *Promise-Giving and Treaty-Making: Homer and*

making and the role of council and assembly in the political sphere,[29] the beginnings of political thinking,[30] warfare and fighting tactics and, more generally, the polis itself.

In particular, recent suggestions concerning early Greek warfare and the evolution of the hoplite phalanx may significantly affect our understanding of the rise of the polis. Mass fighting was long seen as clearly post-Homeric, and the introduction of the phalanx, although based on a long evolution of equipment and tactics, as an event with massive social and political consequences; hence, it was claimed, a "hoplite revolution" around the mid-seventh century ended the phase of elite domination of the polis and ushered in an age of more egalitarian constitutions in which the free farmers played a decisive role.[31]

This view has been challenged by reexamination of battle scenes in the *Iliad* and of hoplite equipment which appears in tombs from ca. 725 and shows characteristics that must have been developed for frontal fighting in dense mass formations.[32] Mass fighting, it now appears, was common much earlier and then made more effective by the development of specific fighting tactics and the appropriate equipment. The phalanx thus developed gradually out of earlier forms of mass fighting. This

---

*the Near East* [Leiden 1992]); Raaflaub, "Politics and Interstate Relations in the World of Early Greek Poleis: Homer and Beyond," *Antichthon* 31 (1997).

[29] E. Havelock, *The Greek Concept of Justice* (Cambridge MA 1978) remains important. See F. Gschnitzer, "Zur homerischen Staats- und Gesellschaftsordnung," in Latacz (n.4) 182-204; Raaflaub, "Homer to Solon: the Rise of the Polis (the Written Evidence)," in Hansen (n.21) 41-105, at 54-56, 67; id. (n.28).

[30] Raaflaub, "Homer and the Beginnings of Political Thought in Greece," in *The Boston Area Colloquium in Ancient Philosophy* 4 (1988) 1-25; "Poets, Lawgivers, and the Beginnings of Political Reflection in Archaic Greece," forthcoming in M. Schofield and C. Rowe (edd), *The Cambridge History of Greek and Roman Political Thought*.

[31] Snodgrass, "The Hoplite Reform and History," *JHS* 85 (1965) 110-22; *Arms and Armour of the Greeks* (London 1967), ch.3; recently, J. Bryant, "Military Technology and Socio-Cultural Change in the Ancient Greek City," *The Sociological Review* 38 (1990) 484-516; Murray (n.12), ch.10; P. Cartledge, in *I Greci* (n.11) II.1, 681-714.

[32] Mass fighting: Pritchett (n.37) IV (1985) 1-93; H. van Wees, "The Homeric Way of War," *G&R* 41 (1994) 1-18, 131-55; "Homeric Warfare," in Morris and Powell (n.4) 668-693; cf. Snodgrass, "The 'Hoplite Reform' Revisited," *DHA* 19 (1993) 47-61, and the chapters by van Wees and S. Mitchell, in A. Lloyd (ed), *Battle in Antiquity* (London 1996). Equipment: chapters by J. Anderson and V. Hanson, in Hanson (ed), *Hoplites* (London 1991).

conclusion corresponds to the fact that communal warfare, depicted amply in the *Iliad*, is attested in Greek historical traditions precisely from the eighth century. Both the theory of a "hoplite revolution" and the related thesis, connecting tyranny and hoplites, that was advanced long ago by Andrewes and Forrest, are thus no longer tenable (see also Starr, 4-5).[33] I have suggested going a step further and connecting the evolution of the phalanx directly with that of the polis: in this view, the polis, the phalanx, and the sphere of "the political" in the polis evolved in an interactive process over a long period of time; the concepts of land ownership and "territoriality" were inseparable components of this interrelated process; and polis aristocracies emerged as part of the same process.[34] Questions certainly remain: for example, what was the ratio in archaic poleis between those who qualified and those who did not? What was the purpose of defining the hoplite class in rigid economic terms, and were such definitions applied universally? Why did the polis not make better military use of its sub-hoplite citizens? Was the phalanx really so uniformly equipped and did light-armed soldiers really play such a marginal role before the late fifth century as is commonly thought?[35]

More generally, the field of ancient Greek military history has long been dominated by studies of military equipment, technology, strategy, and battles.[36] Recently, efforts have been intensified to study warfare and military organization in their broad social, economic, and political context and to understand the ways in which these spheres (and changes in them)

---

[33] A. Andrewes, *The Greek Tyrants* (London 1956) 36-38; W. Forrest, *The Emergence of Greek Democracy* (London 1966) 104-5; *contra*: Snodgrass, "Hoplite Reform" (n.31) 116; C. Starr, *The Economic and Social Growth of Early Greece* (New York 1977) 178-80.

[34] Raaflaub, "Soldiers, Citizens, and the Evolution of the Early Greek Polis," in L. Mitchell and P. Rhodes (edd), *The Development of the Polis in Archaic Greece* (London 1997) 49-59; "War and Society in Archaic and Classical Greece," forthcoming in Raaflaub and N. Rosenstein (edd), *War and Society in the Ancient and Medieval Worlds* (Cambridge MA, in preparation).

[35] J. Anderson, in Grant and Kitzinger (n.11) I, 685-86; J. Ober, "Hoplites and Obstacles," in Hanson, *Hoplites* (n.32) 173-96; H. van Wees, "Politics and the Battle Field," in A. Powell, *The Greek World* (London 1995) 153-78.

[36] E.g., A. Ferrill, *The Origins of War from the Stone Age to Alexander the Great* (London 1985); P. Ducrey, *Warfare in Ancient Greece* (New York 1985); V. Hanson, *The Western Way of War* (New York 1989); *Hoplites* (n.32).

interacted with each other.[37] Such approaches are useful not least for our understanding of the relationship between naval warfare and democracy in fifth-century Athens[38] or of the economic impact of war on the societies involved; for example, Lin Foxhall has recently disputed Victor Hanson's claim that ravaging of the country-side by invading armies had disastrous long-term effects on the polis involved.[39]

Back to the Greek polis. Research on this important topic has reached an entirely new dimension with the establishment of the Copenhagen Polis Center, Mogens Hansen's brainchild. "The Centre's primary aim is to produce a comprehensive inventory of all archaic and classical *poleis*, including colonies, attested in contemporary sources." This inventory will be "accompanied by an in-depth analysis of the origin, nature and development of the *polis*." So far the Center has published three volumes of conference acts and three with articles resulting from the work of its collaborators.[40] The final publication is expected in about four years. The Center's investigation is entirely empirical; its results will establish an immeasurably improved base for future research on the history of the polis, including sharper definitions of concepts such as dependent or autonomous poleis, identifications and locations of poleis, the relation between polis/town and polis/community, between *emporion* and polis, or *kōmē* and polis, the formation of poleis in areas where initially there were none (such as Arkadia), and the combination of poleis into federations.

Others, however, have not been idle. A much better understanding has been reached of the polis in Homer. While

---

[37] W. Pritchett, *The Greek State at War*, 5 vols. (Berkeley 1971-1991); W. R. Connor, "Early Greek Land Warfare as Symbolic Expression," *P&P* 119 (1988) 3-29; Rich and Shipley (n.9); Raaflaub and Rosenstein (n.34).

[38] Below n.87.

[39] V. Hanson, *Warfare and Agriculture in Classical Greece* (Pisa 1983); L. Foxhall, "Farming and Fighting in Ancient Greece," in Rich and Shipley (n.9) 134-45. Generally, Y. Garlan, *Guerre et économie en Grèce ancienne* (Paris 1989); Pritchett (n.37) V (1991), ch.7.

[40] See M. Hansen, "The Copenhagen Inventory of *Poleis*," in Mitchell and Rhodes (n.34) 9-23; Acts: Hansen (ed), *City-State* (n.21); *Sources for the Ancient Greek City-State* (Copenhagen 1995); *Introduction to an Inventory of Poleis* (ibid. 1996). Papers: D. Whitehead (ed), *From Political Architecture to Stephanus Byzantius: Sources for the Ancient Greek Polis* (Stuttgart 1994; cit. 9); M. Hansen and K. Raaflaub (edd), *Studies in the Ancient Greek Polis* (ibid. 1995); *More Studies in the Ancient Greek Polis* (ibid. 1996).

Ehrenberg, Finley, and Starr denied that the Homeric polis was much more than an agglomeration of *oikoi* with, at most, marginal political significance, recent work has established that the epics reflect a form of polis that is very early but essentially contains all components of the polis that are known from the late archaic and classical periods.[41]

When, then, did the polis originate? It may not be possible to give a uniform answer to this question. There certainly were regional differences. Continuity from the Bronze Age may have been stronger, for example, in Crete and Athens than elsewhere, and developments in Ionia may have preceded those on the mainland.[42] Nevertheless, at present the view seems most plausible that the polis as a form of community was decidedly post-Mycenaean; it gradually emerged, often coalescing from small neighboring villages, as a result both of the fragmentation of the Greek world into small local units, typical of the earlier Dark Ages, and of the population increases occurring from the tenth and especially in the eighth century.[43] To what extent Near Eastern models influenced this process remains an open question; the suggestion that the Greeks took the polis over from the Phoenicians certainly is far too simple.[44]

---

[41] V. Ehrenberg, "When Did the Polis Rise?" *JHS* 57 (1937) 147-59, at 155; C. Starr, *Individual and Community: The Rise of the Polis* (New York 1986) 35-36; Finley (n.23) 33-34, 155-56. *Contra*: van Wees (n.24), ch.2; Raaflaub (n.29) 46-59, 75-80.

[42] H. van Effenterre, *La Cité grecque des origines à la défaite de Marathon* (Paris 1985), whose thesis of unbroken continuity from the Bronze Age has not been received favorably; I. Morris, "The Early Polis as City and State," in Rich and Wallace-Hadrill (n.21) 25-57; K.-W. Welwei, *Athen: vom neolithischen Siedlungsplatz zur archaischen Grosspolis* (Darmstadt 1992) 50-75. Ionia: Old Smyrna offers an outstanding example but its date is debated.

[43] E.g., K.-W. Welwei, *Die griechische Polis* (Stuttgart 1983), pts.1-2; "Ursprünge genossenschaftlicher Organisationsformen in der archaischen Polis," *Saeculum* 89 (1988) 12-23; *Athen* (n.42); N. Demand, *Urban Relocation in Archaic and Classical Greece* (Norman OK 1990), chs.2-3; Raaflaub (n.21) 75-82; I. Morris, "Village Society and the Rise of the Greek State," in P. Doukellis and L. Mendoni (edd), *Structures rurales et sociétés antiques* (Paris 1994) 49-53; C. Ampolo, in *I Greci* II.1 (n.11) 297-342. F. Kolb, *Die Stadt im Altertum* (Munich 1984); M. Pallottini, *Alle origini della città europea. Storia dell'urbanistica* (Rome 1993), study the polis in the context of urban development in the ancient world.

[44] M. Bernal, "Phoenician Politics and Egyptian Justice in Ancient Greece," in Raaflaub and Müller-Luckner (n.4) 241-62, cf. ibid. 394-404; see also F. Gschnitzer, "Die Stellung der Polis in der politischen Entwicklung des Altertums," *Oriens antiquus* 27 (1988) 287-302. Starr (n.41) 42 expresses doubts. See, generally, J.

The question then arises how the polis relates to the *ethnos*. Long ago, Fritz Gschnitzer characterized the polis as a local community ("Ortsgemeinde") that developed out of a pre-existing "tribal community" ("Stammesgemeinde"). In some respects this obviously is correct but polis and *ethnos* might also be seen as parallel developments, corresponding to different environments and challenges.[45] The *ethnos* has long been the ancient historians' stepchild. This is now changing rapidly: several teams of scholars are currently investigating a range of *ethnē*, using a broad variety of approaches and all available types of evidence. One of the results emerging from these studies is that *ethnē* often were late constructs, emerging in specific political constellations and supported ideologically by "myths" and genealogies retrojected into a distant past.[46] Let me mention here also a recent increase

---

Davies, "The 'Origins of the Greek *Polis*': Where Should We Be Looking?" in Mitchell and Rhodes (n.34) 24-38.

[45] F. Gschnitzer, "Stammes- und Ortsgemeinden im alten Griechenland," *WS* 68 (1955) 120-44; "Stadt und Stamm bei Homer," *Chiron* 1 (1971) 1-17; for recent discussion, see P. Funke, "Stamm und Polis: Überlegungen zur Entstehung der griechischen Staatenwelt in den 'Dunkeln Jahrhunderten'," in J. Bleicken (ed), *Colloquium...A. Heuss* (Kallmünz 1993) 29-48, and next note.

[46] C. Morgan, "Ethnicity and Early Greek States," *PCPhS* 37 (1991) 131-63; J. Hall, "Approaches to Ethnicity in the Early Iron Age of Greece," in Spencer (n.9) 6-17; id., *Ethnic Identity in Greek Antiquity* (Cambridge 1997); J. McInerney, *The Folds of Parnassos: Land and Ethnicity in Ancient Phokis* (forthcoming); id., "Ethnicity and *Altertumswissenschaft*," forthcoming in D. Tandy (ed), *Political Economy in the Ancient World*; T. Heine Nielsen, "Triphylia: An Experiment in Ethnic Construction and Political Organization," forthcoming; I. Malkin (ed), *Ancient Perceptions of Greek Ethnicity* (in preparation). See also H.-J. Gehrke, "Zwischen Altertumswissenschaft und Geschichte. Zur Standortbestimmung der Alten Geschichte," in E.-R. Schwinge (ed), *Die Wissenschaften vom Altertum am Ende des 2. Jahrtausends n. Chr.* (Stuttgart 1995) 184 n.49. On the state of theoretical research, S. Jones, *Archaeology of Ethnicity* (London 1977), is still useful.

in surveys and histories of regions in mainland Greece[47] as well
as Anatolia and Magna Graecia/Sicily.[48]

The phenomenon of the rise of the polis prompts other
questions. I think of the evolution of political institutions,[49] of
law, civic subdivisions, citizenship,[50] polis religion,[51] and the

---

[47] M. Jameson *et al.*, *A Greek Countryside: the Southern Argolid from Prehistory
to the Present Day* (Stanford 1995); W. Cavanagh *et al.*, *The Laconia Survey* II:
*Archaeological Data. BSA* Suppl. 27 (1996); H.R. Osborne, "Survey and Greek
Society," *AJA* 100 (1996) 165-69, with biblio.; S. Link, *Das griechische Kreta...vom
6. bis zum 4. Jh. v. Chr.* (Stuttgart 1994); P. Berktold *et al.*, *Akarnanien* (Würzburg
1996); Gehrke, in *I Greci* (n.11) 975-94. See id. (n.46) 174 with further bibliography;
E. Olshausen, *Einführung in die historische Geographie der Alten Welt* (Darmstadt
1991), and n.102 below.

[48] Anatolia: e.g., F. Kolb and B. Kupke,*Lykien* (Mainz 1992); further examples in
Gehrke (n.46) 174 n.29. For the western Greeks, see n.10; the relevant chapters in the
new *CAH* and *I Greci* (n.11); R. Holloway, *The Archaeology of Ancient Sicily*
(London 1991), E. De Juliis, *Magna Grecia* (Bari 1996), and the annual *Convegni di
studi sulla Magna Grecia* (Taranto, since 1961).

[49] E.g., Welwei, *Polis* (n.43) 62-75; F. Ruzé, "Les Tribus et la décision politique
dans les cités grecques archaïques et classiques," *Ktema* 8 (1983) 298-306; "*Plethos*:
aux origines de la majorité politique," in *Aux Origines de l'Hellénisme: Hommages à
Henri van Effenterre* (Paris 1984) 247-63; "Basileis, tyrans et magistrats," *Metis* 4
(1989) 211-31; P. Carlier,*La Royauté en Grèce avant Alexandre* (Strasbourg 1984);
"La procédure de décision politique du monde mycénien à l'époque archaïque," in
Musti (n.15) 85-95; E. Stein-Hölkeskamp, *Adelskultur und Polisgesellschaft*
(Stuttgart 1989) 94-103.

[50] U. Walter, *An der Polis teilhaben* (Stuttgart 1992); D. Whitehead, "Norms of
Citizenship in Ancient Greece," in A. Molho *et al.* (edd), *City-States in Classical
Antiquity and Medieval Italy* (Stuttgart and Ann Arbor 1991) 135-54; Athens: P.
Manville, *The Origins of Citizenship in Ancient Athens* (Princeton 1990); A.
Boegehold and A. Scafuro (edd), *Athenian Identity and Civic Ideology* (Baltimore
1994).

[51] J. N. Coldstream, "Greek Temples: Why and Where?" in P. Easterling and J.
Muir (edd), *Greek Religion and Society* (Cambridge 1985) 67-97; W. R. Connor,
"Tribes, Festivals and Processions," *JHS* 107 (1987) 40-50; C. Sourvinou-Inwood,
"What is Polis Religion?" in O. Murray and S. Price (edd), *The Greek City from
Homer to Alexander* (Oxford 1990) 295-322; "Further Aspects of Polis Religion,"
*Annali Istituto Universitario Orientale Napoli* (*AION*) 10 (1988) 259-74; D. Pozzi
and J. Wickersham (edd), *Myth and the Polis* (Ithaca 1991); N. Robertson, *Festivals
and Legends: The Formation of Greek Cities in the Light of Public Ritual* (Toronto
1992); Seaford (n.24); C. Antonaccio, *An Archaeology of Ancestors: Tomb Cult and
Hero Cult in Early Greece* (Lanham MD 1995); F. de Polignac, *Cults, Territory and
the Origins of the Greek City-State* (Chicago 1995); B. Fehr, "The Greek Temple in
the Early Archaic Period," *Hephaistos* 14 (1996) 165-91, and relevant chapters in the
new *CAH* and *I Greci* II.1 (n.11). Athens: n.89. Generally: C. Faraone and D. Obbink

emergence and role of aristocracies and tyrannies.[52] I think
further of institutions facilitating collaboration and interchange
among poleis, such as amphictyonies and symmachies[53] or
regional and panhellenic sanctuaries and games,[54] and of the
relation between the evolution of poleis in the Aegean and that
of poleis in areas "colonized" by the Greeks.[55] Much interesting
work has been done recently on most of these issues; I shall
focus here on only two.

First, the nature and development of civic subdivisions. As
Starr observed (15), the work of Bourriot, published
simultaneously with that of Roussel in 1976, eliminated the
*genos* as the connecting link of a polis structure based
hierarchically on kinship relations. More recently, Nicholas
Jones documented the frequency of similar structural elements
in the world of Greek poleis. The presence of the same four
Ionian and three Doric phylae both in mainland Greece and on
the west coast of Asia Minor suggests an early existence of
these divisions which presumably predate the polis. Others,
however, such as phratries and subdivisions of phratries, seem

(edd), *Magika Hiera: Ancient Greek Magic and Religion* (Oxford 1991); L. Bruit
Zaidman and P. Schmitt Pantel, *Religion in the Ancient Greek City* (Cambridge
1992); D. Lyons, *Gender and Immortality: Heroines in Ancient Greek Myth and Cult*
(Princeton 1997).

[52] W. Donlan, *The Aristocratic Ideal* (Lawrence KA 1980); M. Stahl, *Aristokraten
und Tyrannen im archaischen Athen* (Stuttgart 1987); Stein-Hölkeskamp (n.49); J.
McGlew, *Tyranny and Political Culture in Ancient Greece* (Ithaca 1993); cf. G.
Nagy, E. Stein-Hölkeskamp, in *I Greci* II.1 (n.11). Symposium: O. Murray,
*Sympotica: a Symposium on the Symposion* (Oxford 1990); W. Slater (ed), *Dining in
a Classical Context* (Ann Arbor 1991); P. Schmitt Pantel: *La cité au banquet* (Rome
1992).

[53] K. Tausend, *Amphiktyonie und Symmachie* (Stuttgart 1992); Baltrusch (n.28); P.
Lévêque, in *I Greci* II.1 (n.11) 1111-39.

[54] C. Morgan, *Athletes and Oracles: the Transformation of Olympia and Delphi in
the Eighth Century B.C.* (Cambridge 1990); N. Marinatos and R. Hägg (edd), *Greek
Sanctuaries: New Approaches* (London 1993).

[55] A. Snodgrass, "Interaction by Design: the Greek City-State," in C. Renfrew and
J. Cherry (edd), *Peer Polity Interaction and Socio-Political Change* (Cambridge
1986) 47-58; I. Malkin, *Religion and Colonization in Ancient Greece* (Leiden 1987)
262-66; "Inside and Outside: Colonization and the Formation of the Mother City,"
*AION* (n.51) n.s.1 (1994) 1-9; Raaflaub (n.21) 220-21. On colonization generally, see
n.10 and the relevant chapters in *CAH* III.3² (1982) and *I Greci* II.1 (n.11).

much younger, grown perhaps from neighborhood and cult associations.[56]

Second, the role of law in the evolution of the polis. The traditional view, going back to Aristotle, holds that codification of law was a typical and widespread stage in the evolution of the archaic polis.[57] This view is gradually yielding to another that considers "codification" an unsuitable term, stresses the exceptionality of the enactment of written law, connects it more specifically with the emergence of a political sphere in the polis, and argues that such legislation both presupposes a political will among the citizens and contributes to integrating the community.[58] In particular, K.-J. Hölkeskamp has thoroughly re-examined the evidence for archaic legislation; he demonstrates that large-scale legislation was exceptional, documented only in Athens and Gortyn (and even there we find no systematic or comprehensive law codes). In most cases legislation was limited to single laws or clusters of laws, dealing with a specific set of problems that seriously threatened domestic peace.[59] Draco's law on homicide is an excellent

[56] D. Roussel, *Tribu et cité* (Paris 1976); F. Bourriot, *Recherches sur la nature du genos* (Paris 1976); N. Jones, *Public Organization in Ancient Greece* (Philadelphia 1987); id., *The Associations of Classical Athens* (forthcoming); a different assessment of tribes in McInerney, *The Folds* (n.46); id., in Malkin (n.46); D. Whitehead, *The Demes of Attica* (Princeton 1986); S. Lambert, *The Phratries of Attica* (Ann Arbor 1993; Lambert is now working on subgroups of phratries); J. Davies in *I Greci* II.1 (n.11) 599-652; see also O. Murray, "Cities of Reason," in Murray and Price (n.51) 1-25, and contributions by Murray and M. Piérart in *Acts* IV of the Copenhagen Polis Center (forthcoming, cf. n.40).

[57] M. Gagarin, *Early Greek Law* (Berkeley 1986).

[58] E. Ruschenbusch, "Die Polis und das Recht," in P. Dimakis (ed), *Symposion 1979: Beiträge zur griechischen und hellenistischen Rechtsgeschichte* (Cologne 1983) 305-26; W. Eder, "The Political Significance of the Codification of Law in Archaic Societies," in Raaflaub (ed), *Social Struggles in Archaic Rome* (Berkeley 1986) 262-300; M. Detienne (ed), *Les Savoirs de l'écriture en Grèce ancienne* (Lille 1988), pt.1; H.-J. Gehrke, "Konflikt und Gesetz. Überlegungen zur frühen Polis," in Bleicken (n.45) 49-68; id. (ed), *Rechtskodifikation und soziale Normen im interkulturellen Vergleich* (Tübingen 1994); R. Sealey, *The Justice of the Greeks* (Ann Arbor 1994), ch.2; O. Behrends and W. Sellert (edd), *Nomos und Gesetz* (Göttingen 1995); R. Thomas, "Written in Stone?," in L. Foxhall and A. Lewis (edd), *Greek Law in Its Political Setting* (Oxford 1996) 9-31; G. Camassa, in *I Greci* (n.11) II.1, 561-76.

[59] K.-J. Hölkeskamp, "Written Law in Archaic Greece," *PCPhS* 38 (1992) 87-117; "Arbitrators, Lawgivers and the 'Codification of Law' in Archaic Greece," *Metis* 7

example of this type of legislation.[60] Hölkeskamp's monograph
will contain a comprehensive collection of all testimonia; future
work on this and related issues has further been facilitated by
two recent collections of archaic laws.[61]

The classical polis was a "citizen-state," a *koinōnia
politôn*.[62] Although citizenship was not yet legally defined, this
definition is valid for the early polis as well, especially if the
citizens, as seems now likely, were part of the polis army and
assembly from the very beginning. The matter of citizenship
raises the question, although I cannot discuss it here, of how
membership in this "proto-citizen body" was defined and what
we know both about those who did not meet the criteria and
about other categories of inhabitants: women, slaves, and
foreigners.[63]

## IV

Starr commented on the proliferation of histories of
individual cities (7). This trend seems to have calmed down.[64]
Athens and Sparta, however, continue to stimulate intense
discussions. For Sparta I mention the systematic exploration of
the Laconian countryside, including the perioikic towns and
their territories, undertaken by the British School in Athens,[65] a
recent debate on the impact of the helot problem on Spartan
society, and a new explanation of the Spartan method of voting

---

(1992 [1995]) 49-81; *Schiedsrichter, Gesetzgeber und Gesetzgebung im archaischen
Griechenland* (Stuttgart, forthcoming).

[60] Recently, S. Humphreys, "A Historical Approach to Drakon's Law on
Homicide," in M. Gagarin (ed), *Symposion 1990: Papers on Greek and Hellenistic
Legal History* (Cologne 1991) 17-45.

[61] R. Koerner, *Inschriftliche Gesetzestexte der frühen griechischen Polis* (Cologne
1993); H. van Effenterre and F. Ruzé, *Nomima: Recueil d'inscriptions politiques et
juridiques de l'archaïsme grec*, 2 vols. (Rome 1994-95).

[62] M. Hansen, "The *Polis* as a Citizen-State," in id. (n.21) 7-29.

[63] The citizens presumably were farmers: V. Hanson, *The Other Greeks: The
Family Farm and the Agrarian Roots of Western Civilization* (New York 1995), pt.1;
cf. P. Millett, "Hesiod and His World," *PCPhS* 30 (1984) 84-115. On *thêtes*,
*metanastai*, women and slaves, see summaries and bibliography in Raaflaub,
"Homeric Society" (n.24); cf. further below nn.104-8.

[64] The resumption of excavations at Troy by a joint Tübingen and Cincinnati team
is yielding important information on the long history of this city; see the annual
*Studia Troica* (since 1991) and B. Rose, *Greek and Roman Troy* (in preparation).

[65] See n.47, including a survey by G. Shipley on archaeological sites; cf. id.,
"*Perioikos*: The Discovery of Classical Lakonia," in J. Sanders (ed), *PHILOLAKON:
Lakonian Studies in Honour of Hector Catling* (London 1992) 211-26.

by shouting which turns out to be not primitive as assumed since antiquity but simply based on different assumptions and values.[66] Most important, however, is the ongoing effort, led by Stephen Hodkinson, to reexamine comprehensively the nature and evolution of all that is peculiar about Sparta. Two results seem incrèasingly clear. First, during most of the Archaic period Spartan society was much less exceptional than was commonly held. Its conquests in the eighth century and the helotization of the subjected populations were peculiar responses to challenges that were common in the Hellenic world of the time; the Great Rhetra and heavy reliance on the hoplite farmers were specific and early responses to pressures arising from these developments, but none of this puts Spartan society as early and so much apart from the rest of Greece as was usually believed. Second, the militarization and seclusion of the Spartiate citizens, the ideology of *homoioi* and the educational system of the *agōgē*, retrojected into the mythical past of the founder hero Lycurgus, are late phenomena, developing in the sixth and especially fifth century or even later, consequences of threats experienced or perceived under the pressures of *oliganthrōpia* and the corrupting effects on the elite of Sparta's panhellenic leadership.[67]

As for Athens, the evidence from its early cemeteries, by far the most thoroughly explored in all of the Hellenic world, has stimulated a lively debate, with potentially far-reaching consequences. Observing massive increases in occupation, Snodgrass postulated for the eighth century a veritable population explosion; reacting to criticism, he later modified his view but still insists that the population increase was substantial

---

[66] Helots: R. Talbert, P. Cartledge, *Historia* 38 (1989) 22-40, 40 (1991) 379-89; cf. J. Ducat, *Les Hilotes, BCH* suppl. 20 (1990). Assembly: E. Flaig, "Die spartanische Abstimmung nach der Lautstärke. Überlegungen zu Thukydides 1.87," *Historia* 42 (1993) 139-60.

[67] S. Hodkinson, "Social Order and the Conflict of Values in Classical Sparta," *Chiron* 13 (1983) 239-81; "Inheritance, Marriage and Demography: Perspectives upon the Success and Decline of Classical Sparta," in A. Powell (ed), *Classical Sparta: Techniques behind Her Success* (London 1989) 79-121; "Warfare, Wealth, and the Crisis of Spartiate Society," in Rich and Shipley (n.9) 146-76, and other articles (a book is in preparation); N. Kennell, *The Gymnasium of Virtue: Education and Culture in Ancient Sparta* (Chapel Hill 1995); L. Thommen, *Lakedaimonion politeia* (Stuttgart 1996); cf. M. Nafissi, *La nascita del kosmos* (Naples 1991); P. Cartledge, "Comparatively Equal," in J. Ober and C. Hedrick (edd), *DEMOKRATIA: A Conversation on Democracies, Ancient and Modern* (Princeton 1996) 175-85.

indeed.[68] Ian Morris, taking into account subsequent decreases in occupation of the same cemeteries, explains the evidence differently. His thesis, assuming a series of changes in social values and elite exclusiveness, has the disadvantage of postulating for eighth- and seventh-century Athenian society a development that deviates markedly from all its neighbors.[69] Moreover, Morris argues—correctly, I think—that the early Greek polis was based on a strong egalitarian foundation but his explanation of such equality—a class struggle between *agathoi* and *kakoi* (whom he essentially identifies with *dmōies*, in his view the equivalent of serfs)—is more difficult to accept.[70] I skip recent discussions of Solon, the Peisistratids and Kleisthenes[71] and turn—finally and briefly—to the fifth and fourth centuries.

## V

I shall focus on five points.[72] First, the sources. Commenting on the doubtful reliability of late sources on archaic Greece,

[68] Snodgrass *Archaeology* (n.21) 10-14; *Archaic Greece* (n.19) 21-25; see "Archaeology and the Study of the Greek City" (n.21) 14-16.

[69] I. Morris, *Burial and Ancient Society* (Cambridge 1987); cf. criticism by C. Antonaccio, *AJA* 93 (1989) 296-97; S. Humphreys, *Helios* 17 (1990) 263-68; further bibliography on the controversy in Raaflaub (n.21) 216 n.36; cf. R. Osborne, "A Crisis in Archaeological History? The Seventh Century BC in Attica," *ABSA* 84 (1989) 297-322; Welwei (n.42), pt.2.

[70] Morris (n.69), ch.10; "The Strong Principle of Equality and the Archaic Origins of Greek Democracy," in Ober and Hedrick (n.67) 19-48.

[71] Solon: A. Andrewes, *CAH* III.3² 360-91; Murray (n.12), ch.11; Raaflaub, in *I Greci* (n.11) II.1, 1035-81. Peisistratids: Stein-Hölkeskamp, ibid. 669-76; Andrewes, *CAH* III.3² 392-416; D. Lewis, *CAH* IV² 287-302; Stahl (n.52); cf. H. A. Shapiro, *Art and Cult under the Tyrants in Athens* (Mainz 1989; Supplement 1995). Cleisthenes: M. Ostwald, in *CAH* IV² 303-46; C. Meier, *The Greek Discovery of Politics* (Cambridge MA 1990), ch.4; J. Ober, "The Athenian Revolution of 508/7 B.C.E.," in C. Dougherty and L. Kurke (edd), *Cultural Poetics in Archaic Greece* (Cambridge 1993) 215-32; Raaflaub, "Kleisthenes, Ephialtes und die Begründung der Demokratie," in K. Kinzl (ed), *Demokratia* (Darmstadt 1995) 1-54; N. Loraux, in *I Greci* II.1, 1083-1110. P. Lévêque and P. Vidal-Naquet, *Cleisthenes the Athenian*, now exists in an English transl., augmented by a discussion on the invention of democracy by the authors and C. Castoriadis (Atlantic Highlands NJ 1996).

[72] Handbooks and surveys on the fifth century: E. Will, *Le Monde grec et l'orient* I: *Le V<sup>e</sup> siècle* (Paris 1972), singled out by Starr (9 n.30), still stands out; more recently, M. Ostwald, *From Popular Sovereignty to the Sovereignty of Law* (Berkeley 1986); *CAH* V² (1992); J. Davies, *Democracy and Classical Greece* (Cambridge MA ²1993); C. Meier, *Athen* (Berlin 1993); P. Briant *et al.*, *Le Monde grec aux temps*

Starr wrote, "Down almost to 500 we should rely primarily on the physical evidence, continuously augmented by the archaeologists, and can admit literary sources only if they are really contemporary" (5). What recent research on Herodotus teaches us, confirms this assessment. Whatever we think of the debate on the "liar school of Herodotus,"[73] the historian's narrative is based largely on oral tradition and molded according to his own interests and purposes that have as much, if not more, to do with his own present as with the past.[74] We are losing a historian, at least for the pre-Peisistratid period, but gaining important understanding of the thought processes and cultural contexts by and in which historiography emerged.

The question of oral tradition and oral history as well as the transition from an oral to a literate culture in the Greek world has generally been under intense discussion in the last decade.[75] The recent publication of large fragments of Simonides' elegy on the battle of Plataea offers most interesting new insights, for example, on the heroization of the Persian War dead (important not least as background for the Athenian *patrios nomos*), the relation between myth and history, and that between praise/narrative poetry and historiography (important for our understanding of Thucydides 1.22.4).[76]

*classiques* I: *Le V<sup>e</sup> siècle* (Paris 1995); and forthcoming vols. of *I Greci* (n.11). See also C. Fornara and L. Samons II, *Athens from Cleisthenes to Pericles* (Berkeley 1991); E. Badian, *From Plataea to Potidaea* (Baltimore 1993).

[73] D. Fehling, *Herodotus and His "Sources"* (Leeds 1990); F. Hartog, *The Mirror of Herodotus: the Representation of the Other in the Writing of History* (Berkeley 1988); W. Pritchett, *The Liar School of Herodotus* (Amsterdam 1993).

[74] C. Fornara, *Herodotus* (Oxford 1971) is still important. More recently, D. Boedeker and J. Peradotto (edd), *Herodotus and the Invention of History, Arethusa* 20 (1987); See also J. Marincola, *Authority and Tradition in Ancient Historiography* (Cambridge 1997); Stahl (n.52), pt.I; O. Murray, "Herodotus and Oral History," in *Achaemenid History* (n.8) II (1987) 93-115; J. Gould, *Herodotus* (New York 1989); J. Evans, *Herodotus, Explorer of the Past* (Princeton 1991), and forthcoming works by D. Boedeker (in Boedeker and Raaflaub [n.80]), C. Dewald, R. Thomas.

[75] J. von Ungern-Sternberg and H. Reinau (edd), *Vergangenheit in mündlicher Überlieferung* (Stuttgart 1988); Raaflaub, "Athenische Geschichte und mündliche Überlieferung," ibid. 197-225; W. Harris, *Ancient Literacy* (Cambridge MA 1989); W. Kullmann and M. Reichel (edd), *Der Übergang von der Mündlichkeit zur Literatur bei den Griechen* (Tübingen 1990); R. Thomas, *Oral Tradition and Written Record in Classical Athens* (Cambridge 1989); *Literacy and Orality in Ancient Greece* (ibid. 1992); cf. J. Assmann, *Das kulturelle Gedächtnis* (Munich 1992).

[76] *POxy* 3965; M. West, *Iambi et Elegi Graeci* II² (Oxford 1992) 118ff.; cf. D. Boedeker, "Simonides on Plataea: Narrative Elegy, Mythodic History," *ZPE* 107

In the area of Greek historiography, important work has been done as well on individual authors, placing them and their works in their historical and literary contexts; Xenophon, in particular, finally seems to have stepped out of the shadow of his overpowering predecessor.[77] Equally important is the publication of primary sources, including the continuation of Jacoby's *Fragmente der griechischen Historiker* by Charles Fornara, and the completion of *IG* I³, perhaps the late David Lewis' greatest legacy. Among other epigraphical work, I should single out an article by Mortimer Chambers and colleagues that has given a decisive boost to Harold Mattingly's longstanding effort to down-date many of the Athenian "imperial" decrees.[78] I should mention no less continuing work on the publication of Greek coins and ongoing debates on the origin and function of coinage, as well as Rob Loomis' useful catalogue and interpretation of Athenian monetary figures.[79]

---

(1995) 217-29; ead. and D. Sider (edd), *The New Simonides, Arethusa* 29.2 (1996), with text and bibliography; ead., "Heroic Historiography: Simonides and Herodotus on Plataea," ibid. 223-42. Athens: N. Loraux, *The Invention of Athens* (Cambridge MA 1986).

[77] S. Hornblower, *A Commentary on Thucydides*, 2 vols. (Oxford 1991, 1996); P. Krentz, *Xenophon, Hellenika* (text, transl., comm.), 2 vols. (Warminster 1989, 1995); V. Gray, *The Character of Xenophon's Hellenica* (Baltimore 1989); J. Dillery, *Xenophon and the History of His Times* (London 1995); S. Pomeroy, *Xenophon, Oeconomicus: a Social and Historical Commentary* (Oxford 1994); P. Harding, *Androtion and the Atthis: The Fragments* (transl., comm., Oxford 1994); M. Flower, *Theopompus of Chios* (Oxford 1994); D. Whitehead, *Aineias the Tactician* (transl., comm., Oxford 1990). See also S. Humphreys, "Fragments, Fetishes, and Philosophies: towards a History of Greek Historiography after Thucydides," in G. Most (ed), *Collecting Fragments* (Göttingen 1997) 207-24.

[78] *FGrH* IIIC: *Geschichte von Städten und Völkern*, fasc.1, ed. C. Fornara (Leiden 1994); *IG* I³2, eds. D. Lewis and L. Jeffery (Berlin 1994). M. Chambers *et al.*, "Athens' Alliance with Egesta in the Year of Antiphon," *ZPE* 83 (1990) 38-63; the historical significance is discussed in Chambers' "Foreword" and Mattingly's "Introduction" in H. Mattingly, *The Athenian Empire Restored: Epigraphic and Historical Studies* (Ann Arbor MI 1996), which reprints Mattingly's relevant articles. Other important publications include W. Loomis, *The Spartan War Fund* (Stuttgart 1992); R. Stroud, *The Athenian Law on the Grain-Tax of 374/3 B.C.* (forthcoming as a *Hesperia* suppl.); on other epigraphical work, see Gehrke (n.46) 164 n.7. G. Horsley and J. Lee, "A Preliminary Checklist of Abbreviations of Greek Epigraphic Volumes," *Epigraphica* 56 (1994) 129-65, is very useful.

[79] See T. Martin, *Sovereignty and Coinage in Classical Greece* (Princeton 1985); "Why Did the Greek *Polis* Originally Need Coins?" *Historia* 45 (1996) 257-83 (with earlier bibliograpy); R. Wallace, "The Origin of Electrum Coinage," *AJA* 91 (1987)

Second, frequent calls to overcome "Athenocentrism" are certainly justified but, given the extant evidence, difficult to realize. I already mentioned intensified exploration of *ethnē* and hitherto marginal regions. We now have a useful survey of "The Third Greece" and ample indications that egalitarian developments in the sixth and fifth centuries were not limited to Athens but were a panhellenic if not even wider phenomenon, and that issues we used to consider specifically Athenian and democratic occurred elsewhere in Greece too.[80] Athens, then, remains a special case but was not as completely exceptional as traditionally thought.

Third, such efforts notwithstanding, attention continues to focus on the big powers and polar opposites, Sparta and Athens. As stated before, Sparta is currently a hot topic, with conferences and volumes dedicated to the development of its society and institutions, its imperialism and decline in the late fifth and fourth century, and the attraction it had for thinkers in the classical period.[81] Although we are a little tired of the

---

385-98; I. Carradice (ed), *Coinage and Administration in the Athenian and Persian Empires*, BAR Int. Ser. 343 (Oxford 1987); C. Kraay, in *CAH* IV² 431-45; E. Isik, *Elektronstatere aus Klazomenai* (Saarbrücken 1992); J. Kroll, *The Greek Coins, The Athenian Agora* 26 (Princeton 1993); "Silver in Solon's Laws," forthcoming in R. Ashton *et al.* (edd), *Studies in Greek Numismatics in Memory of M. J. Price* (London 1997); C. Howgego, *Ancient History from Coins* (London 1995); N. Parise, in *I Greci* II.1 (n.11) 715-34. W. Loomis, *Wages, Welfare Costs and Inflation in Classical Athens* (Ann Arbor, forthcoming); *Talents to Chalkoi: A Catalogue of Athenian Monetary Figures* (ibid., forthcoming).

[80] Above nn.46-48; H.-J. Gehrke, *Jenseits von Athen und Sparta. Das Dritte Griechenland und seine Staatenwelt* (Munich 1986); I. Morris, "Strong Principle" (n.70); "Beyond Democracy and Empire: Athenian Art in Context," in D. Boedeker and K. Raaflaub (edd), *Democracy, Empire, and the Arts in Fifth-Century Athens* (in preparation); W. Hoepfner and E.-L. Schwandner, *Haus und Stadt im klassischen Griechenland* (Munich ²1994); W. Schuller and id. (edd), *Demokratie und Architektur* (ibid. 1989); L. Kurke, "The Cultural Impact of (on) Democracy: Decentering Tragedy," forthcoming in I. Morris and K. Raaflaub (edd), *Democracy 2500: Questions and Challenges* (Princeton 1997); E. Robinson, *The First Democracies: Early Popular Government Outside Athens* (Stuttgart 1997).

[81] See nn.65-67. K. Christ (ed), *Sparta* (Darmstadt 1986) includes an introduction on "Spartaforschung und Spartabild" (1-72) and bibliography (471-503). See further Powell (n.67); id. and S. Hodkinson (edd), *The Shadow of Sparta* (London 1994); S. Link, *Der Kosmos Sparta* (Darmstadt 1994); P. Cartledge, *Agesilaos and the Crisis of Sparta* (Baltimore 1987); C. Hamilton, *Agesilaos and the Failure of Spartan Hegemony* (Ithaca 1991; id., *Sparta's Bitter Victories* [Ithaca 1979] remains important); B. Kunstler, "Family Dynamics and Female Power in Ancient Sparta,"

"Athenian miracle" and "Democracy 2500,"[82] and the past decade has not produced a genius "to revolutionize our understanding of the fundamental factors affecting the fifth century" (Starr, 9), a flurry of activity on Athens has yielded interesting and useful results which, however, often concern the fourth century as much as the fifth. For example, although August Boeckh's *Die Staatshaushaltung der Athener* (latest ed. 1886), described by Starr as "the oldest such study on any aspect of Greek history to which we can turn in more than antiquarian interest" (7), has still not been replaced, recent work on the role of finances in Thucydides' thought and in the political reality of late fifth-century Athenian politics, on the administration and economics of naval power, or on Athenian monetary figures offer important first steps toward a new assessment of Athenian public finances.[83] The 2500th anniversary of Cleisthenes' reforms has triggered renewed and wide-ranging debate about the origins of Athenian democracy and the specific historical conditions under which it was possible to develop such an exceptional constitution,[84] how democracy as a whole and its institutions operated,[85] and how it

---

*Helios* 13 (1986) 31-48; M. Dettenhofer, "Die Frauen von Sparta," *Klio* 75 (1993) 61-75; cf. M.-M. Mactoux, in Briant, *Monde grec* (n.72), ch.3.

[82] D. Buitron-Oliver (ed), *The Greek Miracle: Classical Sculpture from the Dawn of Democracy* (Washington DC 1992); R. Osborne and S. Hornblower (edd), *Ritual, Finance, Politics: Athenian Democratic Accounts Presented to David Lewis* (Oxford 1994); W. Coulson *et al.* (edd), *The Archaeology of Athens and Attica under the Democracy* (Oxford 1994); Ober and Hedrick (n.67); Morris and Raaflaub (n.80).

[83] L. Kallet-Marx, *Money, Expense, and Naval Power in Thucydides' History 1-5.24* (Berkeley 1993); *The Uses of Wealth* (in preparation); "Money Talks: Rhetor, Demos, and the Resources of the Athenian Empire," in Osborne and Hornblower (n.82) 227-51; "Accounting for Culture in Fifth-Century Athens," in Boedeker and Raaflaub (n.80); V. Gabrielsen, *Financing the Athenian Fleet* (Baltimore 1994); Loomis (n.79).

[84] Ostwald (n.72); R. Sealey, *The Athenian Republic* (University Park PA 1987); Meier, *Discovery* (n.71), pt.II; *Athen* (n.72); J. Bleicken, *Die athenische Demokratie* (Paderborn ²1994), pt. I; "Wann begann die athenische Demokratie," *HZ* 260 (1995) 337-64; see also Kinzl (n.71), the discussion by Vidal-Naquet *et al.* mentioned in n.71, and various contributions in Morris and Raaflaub (n.80). Fourth century: n.111.

[85] Bleicken, *Demokratie* (n.84) and M. Hansen, *The Athenian Democracy in the Age of Demosthenes* (Oxford 1991) are essential; cf. R. Sinclair, *Democracy and Participation in Athens* (Cambridge 1988); Hansen, *Was Athens a Democracy?* (Copenhagen 1989); J. Ober, *Mass and Elite in Democratic Athens* (Princeton 1989); *The Athenian Revolution* (Princeton 1996); Meier (n.71), ch.6; W. Eder, "Who Rules? Power and Participation in Athens and Rome," in Molho (n.50) 169-96. Councils: P.

dealt with its crisis in the late fifth century.[86] Other studies have focused on relations between democracy and empire or warfare,[87] on democracy, law[88] and religion,[89] on culture and

---

Rhodes, *The Athenian Boule* (Oxford 1972); R. Wallace, *The Areopagos Council to 307 B.C.* (Baltimore 1989). Assembly: Hansen, *The Athenian Assembly* (Oxford 1987); cf. C. Starr, *The Birth of Athenian Democracy: the Assembly in the Fifth Century B.C.* (New York 1990); B. Forsén and G. Stanton (edd), *The Pnyx in the History of Athens* (Helsinki 1996); see also P. Rhodes, *The Decrees of the Greek City-States* (Oxford, forthcoming). Lawcourts: A. Boegehold, *The Lawcourts at Athens, The Athenian Agora* 28 (Princeton 1995).

[86] The 400: A. Andrewes, in A. W. Gomme *et al.*, *A Historical Commentary on Thucydides* V (Oxford 1981) remains essential; cf. id. *CAH* V², ch.11; Ostwald (n.72); Raaflaub, "Politisches Denken und Krise der Polis," *HZ* 255 (1992) 1-60; W. Furley, *Andokides and the Herms* (London 1996). On the Thirty: P. Krentz, *The Thirty at Athens* (Ithaca 1982); T. Loening, *The Reconciliation Agreement of 403/2 B.C. in Athens* (Stuttgart 1987). See further M. Munn, *Athens in the Age of Socrates* (forthcoming); B. Strauss, *Athens after the Peloponnesian War* (Ithaca 1986).

[87] W. Schmitz, *Wirtschaftliche Prosperität, soziale Integration und die Seebundpolitik Athens* (Munich 1988); M. Finley, "War and Empire," in id., *Ancient History: Evidence and Models* (New York 1986) 67-87; C. Meier, "Die Rolle des Krieges im klassischen Athen," *HZ* 251 (1990) 555-605; Raaflaub, "Democracy, Power, and Imperialism in Fifth-Century Athens," in J. Euben *et al.* (edd), *Athenian Political Thought and the Reconstruction of American Democracy* (Ithaca 1994) 103-46; B. Strauss, "The Athenian Trireme, School of Democracy," in Ober and Hedrick (n.67) 313-25; V. Hanson, "Hoplites into Democrats," ibid. 289-312; "Democratic Warfare," in D. McCann and B. Strauss (edd), *Democracy at War* (Washington DC, forthcoming); Raaflaub, "War and Society" (n.34). On naval affairs, see J. Morrison and J. Coates, *The Athenian Trireme* (Cambridge 1986); H. Wallinga, *Ships and Sea-Power before the Great Persian War* (Leiden 1993); Gabrielsen (n.83).

[88] R. Garner, *Law and Society in Classical Athens* (New York 1987); P. Cartledge *et al.* (edd), *Nomos: Essays in Athenian Law, Politics, and Society* (Cambridge 1990); S. Todd, *The Shape of Athenian Law* (Oxford 1993); V. Hunter, *Policing Athens* (Princeton 1994); R. Thomas, "Law and the Lawgiver in the Athenian Democracy," in Osborne and Hornblower (n.82) 119-33; cf. A. Scafuro, *The Forensic Stage* (Cambridge 1997), and, generally, Sealey (n.58); Foxhall and Lewis (n.58).

[89] Essential now: R. Parker, *Athenian Religion: A History* (Oxford 1996); cf. id., "Athenian Religion Abroad," in Osborne and Hornblower (n.82) 339-46; B. Smarczyk, *Untersuchungen zur Religionspolitik und politischen Propaganda Athens im Delisch-Attischen Seebund* (Munich 1990); W. R. Connor, "The Other 399: Religion and the Trial of Socrates," in M. Flower and M. Toher (edd), *Georgica: Greek Studies in Honor of George Cawkwell* (London 1991) 49-56; J. Mikalson, *Honor Thy Gods: Popular Religion in Greek Tragedy* (Chapel Hill 1991); R. Garland, *Introducing New Gods: The Politics of Athenian Religion* (Ithaca 1992); S. Hornblower, "The Religious Dimension to the Peloponnesian War," *HSCP* 94 (1992) 169-97; J. Neils (ed), *Worshipping Athena: Panathenaia and Parthenon* (Madison 1996); M. Jameson, "Democracy and Religion," in Morris and Raaflaub (n.80). See

politics (especially concerning drama, rhetoric, and monuments),[90] city and country,[91] and the role in democracy of elite,[92] oikos and family relations,[93] women and gender relations,[94] and slaves.[95] I confess, though, that I still find the state of our understanding of how specifically democracy

---

generally n.51; P. Hellström and B. Alroth (edd), *Religion and Power in the Ancient Greek World* (Uppsala 1996); Sakellariou (n.90); P. Lévêque, in Briant, *Monde grec* (n.72) 353-83; Powell (n.35), chs.21-23.

[90] Culture: M. Sakellariou (ed), *Démocratie athénienne et culture* (Athens 1996); Boedeker and Raaflaub (n.80); cf. A. Stewart, *Art, Desire, and the Body in Ancient Greece* (Cambridge 1997). Drama: J. Winkler and F. Zeitlin (edd), *Nothing to Do with Dionysos?* (Princeton 1990); C. Meier, *The Political Art of Greek Tragedy* (Baltimore 1993); A. Sommerstein *et al.* (edd), *Tragedy, Comedy and the Polis* (Bari 1993); B. Goff (ed), *History, Tragedy, Theory* (Austin 1995); C. Pelling (ed), *Greek Tragedy and the Historian* (Oxford 1997); S. Saïd, "Tragedy and Politics," in Boedeker and Raaflaub (n.80). Rhetoric: I. Worthington (ed), *Persuasion* (London 1994); H. Yunis, *Taming Democracy* (Ithaca 1996). Monuments: L. Burn, "The Art of the State in Fifth-Century Athens," in M. Mackenzie and C. Roueché (edd), *Images of Authority: Papers...J. Reynolds, PCPhS* Suppl. 16 (1989) 62-81; T. Hölscher, "The City of Athens: Space, Symbol, Structure," in Molho (n.50) 355-80; "Images and Political Identity," in Boedeker and Raaflaub; D. Castriota, *Myth, Ethos, and Actuality: Official Art in Fifth-Century B.C. Athens* (Madison 1992); "Democracy and Art in Late Sixth and Fifth Century Athens," in Morris and Raaflaub (n.80); A. Powell, "Athens' Pretty Face," in Powell (n.35) 245-70.

[91] Murray and Price (n.51); Rich and Wallace-Hadrill (n.21); R. Osborne, *Demos: the Discovery of Classical Attika* (Cambridge 1985); id., (n.102); H. Lohmann, *Atene. Forschungen zur Siedlungs- und Wirtschaftsstruktur des klassischen Attika*, 2 vols. (Cologne 1993).

[92] Donlan (n.52), chs.4-5; Stein-Hölkeskamp (n.49), ch.4; Ober (n.85).

[93] L. Foxhall, "Household, Gender and Property in Classical Athens," *CQ* 39 (1989) 22-44; B. Strauss, *Fathers and Sons in Athens* (Princeton 1993); M. Golden, *Children and Childhood in Classical Athens* (Baltimore 1990); M.-M. Mactoux (n.81) 267-76; cf. n.107.

[94] C. Patterson, "*Hai Attikai*: the Other Athenians," *Helios* 13 (1986) 49-67; R. Just, *Women in Athenian Law and Life* (London 1989); D. Cohen, "Seclusion, Separation, and the Status of Women in Classical Athens," *G&R* 36 (1989) 3-15; *Law, Sexuality, and Society* (Cambridge 1991); E. Keuls, *The Reign of the Phallus* (Berkeley [2]1993); N. Loraux, *The Children of Athena* (Princeton 1993); S. Goldhill, "Representing Democracy: Women at the Great Dionysia," in Osborne and Hornblower (n.82) 347-69; M.-M. Mactoux (n.81) 250-61; cf. n.105.

[95] E. Wood, *Peasant-Citizen and Slave* (London 1988); M. Golden, "The Effects of Slavery on Citizen Households and Children," *Historical Reflections* 15 (1988) 455-75; R. Osborne, "The Economics and Politics of Slavery at Athens," in Powell (n.35) 27-43; M.-M. Mactoux (n.81) 227-42; cf. n.104.

affected the situation of women and slaves somewhat unsatisfactory.[96]

Furthermore, what seems urgently needed now is a comprehensive reexamination of the economic and social transformation of Athens in the fifth century, especially between the Persian and Peloponnesian Wars and during the latter.[97] Such a study could perhaps also give the long-standing debate about the nature of Greek economy new impulses. It seems a priori unlikely that this economy did not change over time. An improved perception of the broad range of relevant phenomena that must have combined with and mutually influenced each other, might help us understand the transition from more rudimentary to more advanced forms of economic behavior and interaction. So far, as Starr observed (15-17), the resulting combination of seemingly incompatible elements—as Sally Humphreys puts it, "not only primitive technology, small-scale organization and a general contempt for economic enterprise, but also wide-spread trade, the beginning of banking and economic analysis, and attitudes characterised by contemporary sources as individualistic and mercenary"[98]—has proved elusive to modern attempts at categorization and resulted in contradictory interpretations.[99]

Fourth, this brings up, more generally, the fields of Greek economic and social history. In both areas it is not easy to separate conditions and developments in the fifth century from those in the fourth (especially since so much of the extant evidence comes from the corpus of fourth-century orators) and

---

[96] The view of S. Pomeroy, *Goddesses, Whores, Wives, and Slaves* (New York 1975) 78, enhanced later by Keuls (n.94), still seems predominant. M. Katz is planning a comprehensive reexamination of the issues involved; see esp. Katz, "Ideology and 'the Status of Women' in Ancient Greece," in Hawley and Levick (n.105) 21-43; L. Foxhall, "Women's Ritual and Men's Work in Ancient Athens," ibid. 97-110; see also J. Winkler, "Phallos Politikos: Representing the Body Politic in Athens," in D. Konstan and M. Nussbaum (edd), *Sexuality in Greek and Roman Society, Differences* 2.1 (1990) 29-45. On slavery, see Osborne (n.95) 34-39.

[97] Preliminary sketches: J. Davies, in *CAH* V² 15-33, 287-305; Raaflaub, "The Transformation of Athens in the Fifth Century," in Boedeker and Raaflaub (n.80).

[98] S. Humphreys, *Anthropology and the Greeks* (London 1978) 137.

[99] See recently P. Millett, *Lending and Borrowing in Ancient Athens* (Cambridge 1991); E. Cohen, *Athenian Economy and Society* (Princeton 1992); see also von Reden (n.25), pts.2-3; I. Morris, "The Athenian Economy Twenty Years after *The Ancient Economy*," *CP* 89 (1994) 351-66; S. Meikle, "Modernism, Economics, and the Ancient Economy," *PCPhS* 41 (1995) 174-91; further below n.126.

what is generally valid from what is specifically Athenian. Given the amount of activity in both fields, it is remarkable that the space attributed to them in recent comprehensive histories of the Greek world (*The Cambridge Ancient History* and *I Greci*), compared to political history, is still very small. As far as the economy is concerned, the great debate about its general character, just mentioned, tends to overshadow other useful discussions of the whole and individual aspects.[100] Here I should also point to efforts to situate culture and warfare in their economic contexts[101] and to pay attention to the "rural Greek past"[102] as well as ecology and agriculture.[103] Overall, though, at least partly due to the differences in quantity and nature of the

---

[100] Generally, P. Garnsey *et al.* (edd), *Trade in the Ancient Economy* (Berkeley 1983); L. Casson, *Ancient Trade and Society* (Detroit 1984); H. Kloft, *Die Wirtschaft der griechisch-römischen Welt* (Darmstadt 1992); Davies (n.97); M. Austin, in *CAH* VI² 527-64; J. Andreau *et al.* (edd), *Les échanges dans l'Antiquité: le rôle de l'Etat* (Saint-Bertrand-de-Comminges 1994); R. Ducat, in Briant, *Monde grec* (n.72) 295-352; P. Cartledge, "'The Economy (Economies) of Ancient Greece," forthcoming in *Dialogos* 5 (1998). On particular issues, e.g., R. Meiggs, *Trees and Timber in the Ancient Mediterranean* (Oxford 1982); L. Migeotte, *L'Emprunt public dans les cités grecques* (Paris 1984); R. Descat, *L'Acte et l'effort. Une idéologie du travail en Grèce ancienne* (Paris 1986); P. Garnsey, *Famine and Food Supply in the Graeco-Roman World* (Cambridge 1988); C. Whittaker (ed), *Pastoral Economies in Classical Antiquity* (Cambridge 1988); S. Mrozek, *Lohnarbeit im klassischen Altertum* (Bonn 1989); S. Meikle, *Aristotle's Economic Thought* (Oxford 1995).

[101] L. Kurke, *The Traffic in Praise: Pindar and the Poetics of Social Economy* (Ithaca 1991); "The Economy of Kudos," in Dougherty and Kurke (n.71) 131-63; Kallet-Marx, "Accounting for Culture" (n.83). Warfare: Gabrielsen (n.83); Garlan (n.39), Pritchett (n.37); P. Millett, "Warfare, Economy, and Democracy in Classical Athens," in Rich and Shipley (n.9) 177-96.

[102] H. van Andel Tjeerd and C. Runnels, *Beyond the Acropolis: a Rural Greek Past* (Stanford 1987); R. Osborne, *Classical Landscape with Figures: The Ancient Greek City and Its Countryside* (London 1987); Snodgrass (n.18), chs.3-4; Murray and Price (n.51), chs.4-7; Rich and Wallace-Hadrill (n.21); S. Alcock *et al.*, "Intensive Survey, Agricultural Practice and the Classical Landscape of Greece," in Morris (n.7) 137-70; N. Spencer, "Multi-Dimensional Group Definition in the Landscape of Rural Greece," in Spencer (n.9) 28-41; see also n.91.

[103] C. R. Whittaker (ed), *Pastoral Economies in Classical Antiquity, PCPhS* Suppl. 14 (1988); R. Sallares, *The Ecology of the Ancient Greek World* (Ithaca 1991); G. Shipley and J. Salmon (edd), *Human Landscapes in Classical Antiquity* (London: 1996); T. Gallant, *Risk and Survival in Ancient Greece* (Stanford 1991); B. Wells (ed), *Agriculture in Ancient Greece* (Stockholm 1992); S. Isager and J. Skydsgaard, *Ancient Greek Agriculture* (London 1992); A. Burford, *Land and Labor in the Greek World* (Baltimore 1993), and in CAH VI2 661-77; Hanson (n.63); B. Bravo, in *I Greci* (n.11) 527-60.

extant evidence, interest in and understanding of Greek economic history seem to lag behind its Roman counterpart. In the field of social history, work on slavery and other underprivileged groups or outsiders, such as foreigners or the disabled, and on social policies continues.[104] Most importantly, however, the pioneering work begun long ago by scholars such as Sarah Pomeroy and Marilyn (Arthur) Katz has grown into full blossom. Surveys and collected volumes abound on women's history,[105] and valuable work has been appearing on the application of feminist theory to the classics and on various aspects of sexuality,[106] the family,[107] and the ways various Greek authors dealt with these issues.[108]

---

[104] M. Finley (ed), *Classical Slavery* (London 1987); Y. Garlan, *Slavery in Ancient Greece* (Ithaca 1988); N. Fisher, *Slavery in Classical Greece* (Bristol 1993); *"Hybris, Status and Slavery,"* in Powell (n.35) 44-84; Cartledge (n.10), ch.6; E. Meyer, *Manumission and the Evolution of Slavery in Greece, 700 BC-AD 350* (in preparation); R. Lonis (ed), *L'Etranger dans le monde grec*, 2 vols. (Nancy 1988, 1992); Cartledge, ch.5; H. Kloft (ed), *Sozialmassnahmen und Fürsorge* (Graz 1988); R. Garland, *The Eye of the Beholder: Deformity and Disability in the Graeco-Roman World* (Ithaca 1995); M. Dillon, "Payments to the Disabled at Athens: Social Justice or Fear of Aristocratic Patronage?" *AncSoc* 26 (1995) 27-57.

[105] P. Culham, "Ten Years after Pomeroy: Studies of the Image and Reality of Women in Antiquity," *Helios* 13 (1986) 9-30; R. Sealey, *Women and Law in Classical Greece* (Chapel Hill 1990); P. Schmitt Pantel (ed), *A History of Women in the West* I (Cambridge MA 1992); Cartledge (n.10), ch.4; M. DeForest (ed), *Woman's Power, Man's Game: Essays...J. King* (Wauconda IL 1993); N. Demand, *Birth, Death, and Motherhood in Classical Greece* (Baltimore 1994); E. Fantham *et al., Women in the Classical World* (New York 1994); S. Blundell, *Women in Ancient Greece* (Cambridge MA 1995); R. Hawley and B. Levick (edd), *Women in Antiquity* (London 1995); E. Reeder (ed), *Pandora: Women in Classical Greece* (Baltimore and Princeton 1995).

[106] N. Rabinowitz and A. Richlin (edd), *Feminist Theory and the Classics* (London 1993). J. Winkler, *The Constraints of Desire: The Anthropology of Sex and Gender in Ancient Greece* (London 1990); D. Halperin, *One Hundred Years of Homosexuality and Other Essays on Greek Love* (London 1990); id. *et al.* (edd), *Before Sexuality: The Construction of Erotic Experience in the Ancient Greek World* (Princeton 1990); E. Cantarella, *Bisexuality in the Ancient World* (New Haven 1992); A. Richlin (ed), *Pornography and Representation in Greece and Rome* (New York 1992); C. Reinsberg, *Ehe, Hetärentum und Knabenliebe im antiken Griechenland* (Munich 1993); W. Percy III, *Pederasty and Pedagogy in Archaic Greece* (Urbana IL 1996); A. Kolowski-Ostrow and C. Lyons (edd), *Naked Truths: Women, Sexuality and Gender in Classical Art and Archaeology* (London 1997); S. Deacy and K. Pierce (edd), *Rape in Antiquity* (London 1997).

[107] J. Martin, "Zur Stellung des Vaters in antiken Gesellschaften," in H. Süssmuth (ed), *Historische Anthropologie. Der Mensch in der Geschichte* (Göttingen 1984) 84-

Fifth and finally, Starr found that in the mid-1980s the fourth century was still conventionally seen as an "era of gloom and decay after the glories of the age of Pericles" (9). Although this view still has its adherents,[109] and the fourth century probably still occupies a position of transition between two more clearly defined periods, major progress has been made toward a more balanced assessment. Walter Eder's volume on fourth-century Athenian democracy explicitly tackles the issue of "climax or decline,"[110] and several other collected volumes offer thoughtful new assessments.[111] Many problems, some of which Starr pointed out as being in need of attention, have received thorough treatment, for example, the Greek condottieri generals (especially Agesilaos) and the relation between citizen soldiers and mercenaries, as well as other problems related to warfare,[112] the phenomenon of *stasis* in the Greek world,[113] the

---

109; id. and A. Nitschke, *Zur Sozialgeschichte der Kindheit* (Freiburg 1986); id. and R. Zoepffel (edd), *Aufgaben, Rollen und Räume von Frau und Mann* (Munich 1989); I. Weiler, "Witwen und Waisen im griechischen Altertum," in Kloft (n.104) 15-33; M. Golden, "Continuity, Change and the Study of Ancient Childhood," *Classical Views* 36 (1992) 7-18; L.-M. Günther, "Witwen in der griechischen Antike," *Historia* 42 (1993) 308-25; S. Humphreys, *The Family, Women and Death* (Ann Arbor [2]1993); G. Giglioni, in *I Greci* II.1 (n.11) 735-54; D. Ogden, *Greek Bastardy in the Classical and Hellenistic Periods* (Oxford 1996); S. Pomeroy, *Families in Classical and Hellenistic Greece* (Oxford 1997); C. Patterson, *The Family in Greek History* (forthcoming).

[108] S. des Bouvrie, *Women in Greek Tragedy: An Anthropological Approach* (Oslo 1990); A. Powell (ed), *Euripides, Women, and Sexuality* (London 1990); N. Rabinowitz, *Anxiety Veiled: Euripides and the Traffic in Women* (Ithaca 1993); L. Taaffe, *Aristophanes and Women* (London 1993); cf. F. Zeitlin, *Playing the Other: Gender and Society in Classical Greek Literature* (Chicago 1996).

[109] E.g., W. Runciman, "Doomed to Extinction: The *Polis* as an Evolutionary Dead-End," in Murray and Price (n.51) 347-67; a more positive view in Strauss (n.86) 42-69; A. French, "Economic Conditions in Fourth-Century Athens," *G&R* 38 (1991) 24-40.

[110] W. Eder (ed), *Die athenische Demokratie im 4. Jh. v. Chr.: Vollendung oder Verfall einer Verfassungsform?* (Stuttgart 1995); cf. Hansen, *Assembly* and *Democracy*; Ober, *Mass and Elite* (all n.85); Bleicken, *Demokratie* (n.84).

[111] *CAH* VI[2] (1994); P. Carlier (ed), *Le IVe siècle av. J. C.* (Nancy 1996); L. Tritle (ed), *The Greek World in the Fourth Century* (London 1997).

[112] Cartledge, Hamilton (both n.81); L. Burckhardt, *Bürger und Soldaten* (Stuttgart 1996); M. Munn, *The Defense of Attica* (Berkeley 1993; cf. J. Ober, *Fortress Attica* [Leiden 1985]); J. Heskel, *The North-Aegean War, 371-360 BC* (Stuttgart 1997).

development and rising prominence of federal states,[114] or Athenian statesmen and politics of the fourth century.[115] Understanding of Macedonian history and politics has been advanced by fundamental studies on many issues, and the Persian side as well is much better illuminated today than it was ten years ago.[116]

## VI

Other areas of historical research could be treated as well, such as science,[117] medicine,[118] and technology,[119] mentalité,[120]

---

[113] Whitehead (n.77); cf. H.-J. Gehrke, *Stasis* (Munich 1985); N. Loraux, "Reflections of the Greek City on Unity and Division," in Molho (n.50) 33-51; T. Figueira, "A Typology of Social Conflict in Greek Poleis," ibid. 289-307.

[114] G. Daverio Rocchi, *Città-Stato e Stati federali della Grecia classica* (Milan 1993) repeats long-standing prejudices; H. Beck, *Polis und Koinon* (Stuttgart 1997) offers a good summary. See also n.46 above.

[115] S. Humphreys, "Lycurgus of Butadae: an Athenian Aristocrat," in J. Eadie and J. Ober (edd), *The Craft of the Ancient Historian: Essays...C. Starr* (Lanham MD 1985) 199-252; L. Tritle, *Phocion the Good* (London 1988); R. Sealey, *Demosthenes and His Time: A Study in Defeat* (New York 1993); J. Engels, *Studien zur politischen Biographie des Hypereides* (Munich ²1993); E. Harris, *Aeschines and Athenian Politics* (New York 1995); see also J. Trevett, *Apollodorus the Son of Pasion* (Oxford 1992).

[116] Macedonia: E. Borza, *In the Shadow of Olympus: The Emergence of Macedon* (Princeton 1990); J. Heskel, "Macedonia and the North, 400-336," in Tritle (n.111) 167-88; for further bibliography, see Burstein's chapter in the present vol.; Persia: above n.8; S. Ruzicka, *Politics of a Persian Dynasty. The Hecatomnids in the 4th century B.C.* (Norman OK 1992); S. Hornblower, in *CAH* VI² 45-96.

[117] G. Lloyd, *The Revolutions of Wisdom* (Berkeley 1987); *Methods and Problems in Greek Science* (Cambridge 1991); *Adversaries and Authorities: Investigations into Ancient Greek and Chinese Science* (Cambridge 1996); A. Pichot, *La Naissance de la Science* (Paris 1991); R. French, *Ancient Natural History* (London 1994); L. Zhmud, *Wissenschaft, Philosophie und Religion im frühen Pythagoreismus* (Berlin, 1997).

[118] J. Longrigg, "Presocratic Philosophy and Hippocratic Medicine," *Hist Sci* 27 (1989) 1-39; *Greek Rational Medicine* (London 1993); M. Grmek, *Diseases in the Ancient Greek World* (Baltimore 1989).

[119] D. Hill, *A History of Engineering in Classical and Medieval Times* (London 1984); P. Keyser, "Alchemy in the Ancient World: From Science to Magic," *ICS* 15 (1990) 353-78; D. Hägermann and H. Schneider, *Propyläen Technikgeschichte: Landbau und Handwerk, 750 v. Chr. bis 1000 n. Chr.* (Berlin 1991); H. Schneider, *Das griechische Technikverständnis* (Darmstadt 1989); *Einführung in die antike Technikgeschichte* (Darmstadt 1992); R. Tölle-Kastenbein, *Das archaische Wasserleitungsnetz für Athen* (Mainz 1994); T. Rihll and J. Tucker, "Greek Engineering: the Case of Eupalinos' Tunnel," in Powell (n.35) 403-31.

[120] E.g., C. Meier, "Die Angst und der Staat. Fragen und Thesen zur Geschichte menschlicher Affekte," in H. Rössner (ed), *Der ganze Mensch. Aspekte einer*

the social function of sports,[121] the *Nachleben* of ancient traditions and their influences on later periods[122] as well as *Wissenschaftsgeschichte*,[123] but enough is enough.

I end by touching briefly upon a problem that should be of concern not only but especially to all ancient historians. It was raised by Starr (14-17) and has to do with theory and "interdisciplinarity." Both figure prominently in the scholarship of the last decade. No doubt, despite the decline of Marxism, both in political ideology and historical theory,[124] theoretical and interdisciplinary awareness among ancient historians is increasing steadily.[125] Through the work of members of the "French School," founded by Jean-Pierre Vernant, and what we might call the "Cambridge School," led by Moses Finley and Anthony Snodgrass, and scholars in many countries inspired by them, among others, the approaches of social, economic and

---

*pragmatischen Anthropologie* (Munich 1996) 228-46; G. Lloyd, *Demystifying Mentalities* (Cambridge 1990); H.-J. Gehrke, "Die Griechen und die Rache. Ein Versuch in historischer Psychologie," *Saeculum* 38 (1987) 121-49; E. David, "Laughter in Spartan Society," in Powell, *Classical Sparta* (n.67) 1-25.

[121] M. Poliakoff, *Combat Sports in the Ancient World* (New Haven 1987); M. Golden, *Sport and Society in Ancient Greece* (Cambridge, forthcoming).

[122] M. Reinhold, *Classica Americana* (Detroit 1984); P. Rahe, *Republics Ancient and Modern* (Chapel Hill 1992); S. Wiltshire, *Greece, Rome, and the Bill of Rights* (Norman OK 1992); C. Richard, *The Founders and the Classics* (Cambridge MA 1994); J. Roberts, *Athens on Trial: The Antidemocratic Tradition in Western Thought* (Princeton 1994); C. Mossé, *L'Antiquité dans la révolution française* (Paris 1989); P. Vidal-Naquet, *La Démocratie grecque vue d'ailleurs* (Paris 1990).

[123] K. Christ, *Von Gibbon zu Rostovtzeff. Leben und Werk führender Althistoriker der Neuzeit* (Darmstadt ³1989); *Neue Profile der Alten Geschichte* (Darmstadt 1990); W. Briggs and W. Calder III (edd), *Classical Scholarship: A Biographical Encyclopaedia* (New York 1990); W. Calder III and A. Demandt (edd), *Eduard Meyer* (Leiden 1990); M. Wes, *Michael Rostovtzeff: Historian in Exile* (Stuttgart 1990); W. Calder and S. Trzaskoma (edd), *George Grote Reconsidered* (Hildesheim 1996): E. Badian (ed), *In Memory of Fritz Schachermeyr*, *AJAH* 13.1 (1988 [1996]), and works on the role of ancient history and ancient historians in Germany before and after World War II, listed by Gehrke (n.46) 188 nn.63, 65.

[124] But see P. Cartledge and D. Konstan, "Marxism and Classical Antiquity," *OCD*³ 933-34; P. Rose, *Sons of the Gods, Children of Earth: Ideology and Literary Form in Ancient Greece* (Ithaca 1992) 1-42; id., in Rabinowitz and Richlin (n.106), ch.9.

[125] See relevant chapters in P. Culham and L. Edmunds (edd), *Classics: A Discipline and Profession in Crisis?* (Lanham MD 1989); H. Hansen and J. Peradotto (edd), *Rethinking the Classical Canon, Arethusa* 27.1 (1994); *The "Crisis" Revisited, CW* 89.1 (1995); "Classics and Comparative Literature: Agenda for the '90s," *CP* 92 (1997) 153-88.

cultural anthropology, sociology, and political science[126] as well
as new methods in archaeology[127] have had an increasing and,
on the whole, stimulating and beneficial influence on research
in ancient history. To mention only a few examples, I think of
renewed interest in Max Weber's sociology of the city and its
applicability to the ancient city as well as continued work along
the lines of Finley's work on the ancient city,[128] the enormous
impact of anthropology on gender studies,[129] the influence of
political science and theory of history on analyses of Athenian
democracy and its prehistory,[130] or of "cultural poetics" or "new
historicism," a vague but increasingly popular methodology that
aims at overcoming the separation between literary text and

---

[126] See generally, Humphreys (n.98); M. Finley, "Anthropology and the Classics,"
in id., *The Use and Abuse of History* (London 1975) 102-19; J. Redfield, "Classics
and Anthropology," *Arion* 3rd ser. 1.2 (1991) 5-23; W. Nippel, "Die Heimkehr der
Argonauten aus der Südsee. Ökonomische Anthropologie und die Theorie der
griechischen Gesellschaft in klassischer Zeit," *Chiron* 12 (1992) 1-39; id., *Griechen,
Barbaren und "Wilde." Alte Geschichte und Sozialanthropologie* (Frankfurt am Main
1990); D. Tandy and W. Neale, "Karl Polanyi's Distinctive Approach to Social
Analysis and the Case of Ancient Greece," in C. Duncan and D. Tandy (edd), *From
Political Economy to Anthropology: Situating Economic Life in Past Societies*
(Montreal 1994) 9-33. See also Gehrke (n.46) 160-96, and T. Hölscher, "Klassische
Archäologie am Ende des 20. Jahrhunderts: Tendenzen, Defizite, Illusionen," in
Schwinge (n.46) 197-228.
[127] See, e.g., Snodgrass, *An Archaeology of Greece* (n.18); Morris, *Classical
Greece* (n.7); id., "Archaeologies of Greece," ibid. 8-47; "Periodization and the
Heroes" (n.17); Michael Shanks, *Classical Archaeology of Greece* (London 1996).
[128] Finley, "The Ancient City: From Fustel de Coulanges to Max Weber and
beyond," in id. (n.16), ch.1; cf. B. Shaw and R. Saller, "Editors' Introduction," ibid.
ix-xxvi; *La Cité antique? A partir de l'oeuvre de M. I. Finley, Opus* 6-8 (1987-89).
On Max Weber, W. Nippel, "Max Weber's 'The City' Revisited," in Molho (n.50)
19-30; "Vom Nutzen und Nachteil Max Webers für die Althistorie," *A&A* 40 (1994)
169-80; "Republik, Kleinstaat, Bürgergemeinde. Der antike Stadtstaat in der
neuzeitlichen Theorie," in P. Blickle (ed), *Theorien kommunaler Ordnung in Europa*
(Munich 1996) 225-47; C. Meier (ed), *Die Okzidentale Stadt nach Max Weber*
(Munich 1994).
[129] E.g., Des Bouvrie (n.108); Winkler, *Constraints* (n.106); Humphreys, *Family*
(n.107); Just (n.94), writing "as a social anthropologist rather than as an ancient
historian or a classicist." See also Rabinowitz and Richlin (n.106).
[130] C. Meier, "Autonomprozessuale Zusammenhänge in der Vorgeschichte der
griechischen Demokratie," in id. and K.-G. Faber (edd), *Historische Prozesse*
(Munich 1978) 221-47; *Introduction à l'anthropologie politique de l'Antiquité
classique* (Paris 1984); id., *Discovery* (n.71), chs.4, 6; Ober and Hedrick (n.67);
Euben (n.87); id. (ed), *Greek Tragedy and Political Theory* (Berkeley 1986).

cultural as well as material context.[131] Interdisciplinary work is much more normal today than it was even a decade or two ago, both within the discipline of classics where students of history and literature pay closer attention to each other and to the evidence of material culture, and beyond the boundaries of the discipline, in collaborative ventures between classicists and scholars in the social sciences, Near Eastern and religious studies, and others.[132]

All this is very positive, but problems persist. To cite only one, despite such efforts to bridge "the great divide," the divide is still there, deep and often frustrating. It operates both within and outside the discipline of classical studies. I think of tendencies in universities and professional organizations to separate archaeology from more text-based classical studies, tendencies that are understandable because of the different methodologies and constituencies involved but, in my view, detrimental to all sides. More generally, the differences separating the classics (including Old World archaeology and ancient history), for example, from political science or New World archaeology/anthropology are still profound, hampering fruitful communication and collaboration. Our discipline—with its traditional focus on evidence that, despite new discoveries, is finite and has often been analyzed a hundred times over, with its finely honed methodologies, highly developed sense of historical evolution and its long and distinguished but not unproblematic tradition (the shifting role of classics in education with its intimate ties to the vicissitudes of social and political changes in the last two centuries)[133]—this discipline

[131] Dougherty and Kurke (n.71); on "cultural poetics," see "Introduction," ibid. 1-12, and *APA Newsletter* 17.5 (Oct. 1994) 11-12; further examples: Kurke (n.101); Sourvinou-Inwood, *'Reading' Greek Death* (Oxford 1995); *'Reading' Greek Culture: Texts and Images, Rituals and Myths* (Oxford 1991); D. Lyons, "The Economics of Gender: Women and Exchange in Ancient Greece" (in preparation).

[132] See, e.g., Ober and Hedrick (n.67); Raaflaub and Müller-Luckner (n.4); K. Irani and M. Silver (edd), *Social Justice in the Ancient World* (Westport CT 1995). Molho *et al.* (n.50) represents an effort to stimulate collaboration between ancient and medieval historians. I hope that such collaborative efforts will continue.

[133] E.g., B. Knox, *The Oldest Dead White European Males and Other Reflections on the Classics* (New York 1993); G. Kennedy, "Shifting Visions of Classical Paradigms," *IJCT* 1 (1994) 7-16; J. Latacz, "Die Gräzistik der Gegenwart," in Schwinge (n.46) 41-89, at 45-58. For classical studies in the U.S., see M. Reinhold, *Classica Americana* (Detroit 1984), including G. Kennedy, "An Essay on Classics in America since the Yale Report" (325-51).

does not find it all that easy to communicate constructively with representatives of fields that speak different scholarly languages, operate from a strong and explicit theoretical foundation throughout, drown in evidence or, conversely, lack textual evidence (almost) completely, and often show a poor understanding of the importance of the historical dimension.[134] Only patient work on both sides, discussions perhaps in small workshops rather than large conferences, collaboration on specific topics and problems, and consistent encouragement of graduate students to pay attention to a wide variety of approaches will eventually succeed in overcoming these obstacles. That such patient work, on the part of as many individuals as possible, is vital for the future of our discipline can hardly be emphasized enough.[135]

---

[134] See, for example, the discussion between D. Small and I. Morris, in Morris and Raaflaub (n.80). See also D. Small (ed), *Methods in the Mediterranean: Historical and Archaeological Views on Texts and Archaeology* (Leiden 1995); Spencer (n.9).

[135] For a historical perspective on the ancient historian's task, see W. Nippel (ed), *Über das Studium der Alten Geschichte* (Munich 1993), with statements from von Humboldt and Niebuhr to A. Heuss and C. Meier.

# II

## THE HELLENISTIC AGE

*Stanley M. Burstein*

## HELLENISTIC HISTORIOGRAPHY

Hellenistic history has long been the step-child of Greek historiography. Already in the second century A.D. Pausanias (1.6.1) noted the lack of interest in the history of the Hellenistic kingdoms. Not surprisingly, few Hellenistic histories survived into the Middle Ages. Indeed, the ninth century A.D. classical scholar and Patriarch of Constantinople Photius knew only three such works, Books 17-40 of Diodorus' *Library of History* and Arrian's and Dexippus' histories of the Diadochoi. Although palimpsest fragments of a copy of Arrian's *Ta meta Alexandron* have been discovered in the scattered remains of a manuscript that was brought to Italy in the high middle ages,[1] no complete copies of these works survived the Turkish conquest. Nor did the publication in the late eighteenth and early nineteenth century of pioneering histories of the Hellenistic monarchies by John Gast[2] and John Gillies[3] change this situation. Only in the middle and late nineteenth century did significant scholarly interest in the Hellenistic period appear. Three factors were responsible for this development.

---

[1] For the most recent discovery, see Jacques Noret, "Un fragment du dixième livre de la Succession d'Alexandre par Arrien retrouvé dans un palimpsest de Gothenburg," *AC* 52 (1983) 235-242; and Stephen Schröder, "Zum Göteborger Arrian-Palimpsest," *ZPE* 71 (1988) 75-90.

[2] John Gast, *The History of Greece, from the accession of Alexander of Macedon, till its final subjection to the Roman power* (London 1782).

[3] John Gillies, *The History of the World from the Reign of Alexander to that of Augustus*, 2 vols. (London 1807).

The first was the publication between 1833 and 1843 of the first edition of J. G. Droysen's great three volume *Geschichte des Hellenismus,* with its revolutionary interpretation of the Hellenistic period as the time in which Greek and Near Eastern cultures mingled in the lands conquered by Alexander the Great to form the cultural matrix from which Christianity emerged.[4] The second was the discovery in Egypt of large quantities of both literary and nonliterary papyri. These new texts have made the nineteenth and twentieth centuries the most important period for the recovery of classical literature since the Renaissance. Equally important, they also provided scholars with a remarkably detailed view of the government and society of a major kingdom, Ptolemaic Egypt. The third was the creation of new European empires in the areas once dominated by the Hellenistic kingdoms, which opened these regions to Western exploration while encouraging scholars to see Alexander, his Macedonian successors, and their Greek collaborators as forerunners of their own countrymen and their imperial endeavors. For the first time since antiquity, Hellenistic history had become "relevant". The result was almost a century of creative scholarship in which three generations of talented historians assimilated the new data and fleshed out Droysen's view of Hellenistic civilization as a mixed culture, Greek in its essential character but enriched by the admixture of elements derived from the ancient cultures of the Near East.

The "heroic age" of Hellenistic scholarship ended shortly after World War II. To be sure, major works in the great tradition of Hellenistic scholarship continued to appear during the next few decades. Frank Walbank's indispensable commentary on Polybius,[5] P. M. Fraser's massive account of Hellenistic Alexandria,[6] N.G.L. Hammond's *A History of Macedonia,*[7] and the comprehensive histories of Édouard Will[8] and Claire Préaux[9] are obvious examples. Still, these works

---

[4] Cf. A. D. Momigliano, "J. G. Droysen Between Greeks and Jews," *History and Theory* 9 (1970) 139-153.

[5] Frank L. Walbank, *A Historical Commentary on Polybius*, 3 vols. (Oxford 1957-1979).

[6] P. M. Fraser, *Ptolemaic Alexandria*, 3 vols. (Oxford 1972).

[7] N. G. L. Hammond *et al.*, *A History of Macedonia*, 3 vols. (Oxford 1972-1988).

[8] Édouard Will, *Histoire Politique du Monde Hellénistique 323-30 av. J.-C.* 2 vols., 2nd. ed. (Nancy 1979-1982).

[9] Claire Preaux, *Le Monde Hellénistique: La Grèce et l'Orient (323-146 av. J.-C.)* 2 vols. (Paris 1978).

stand out as isolated peaks of scholarly achievement in a period marked by a steep decline in interest in Hellenistic history.

Starr (20)[10] accurately summed up the state of Hellenistic scholarship in the 1970's and 1980's when he quoted approvingly E. Olshausen's observation that "modern research on the Hellenistic Period has not been blessed with historical monographs." A similar impression emerges from the survey of Hellenistic studies I compiled for the library journal *Choice* in 1990.[11] With some justice, however, Starr and I might have echoed King Louis XV of France and observed that "*après nous le déluge*," for the last decade has seen a veritable flood of new works devoted to Hellenistic studies.

The first signs of the new wave of Hellenistic scholarship were already evident when Starr's survey appeared in the late 1980's. Conferences devoted to Hellenistic themes had begun to proliferate both in the United States and abroad as did the volumes of their proceedings.[12] Research projects with Hellenistic emphases also were established. In Europe the Danish Council for the Humanities established a multi-year research project on Hellenistic society and culture[13] while in the United States Duke University in collaboration with the Packard Humanities Institute undertook to make available in electronic form all hitherto published documentary papyri. More recently, the University of California, Berkeley has announced plans to complete the long delayed publication of the Tebtunis Papyri. The monograph deficit noted by Starr also began to be remedied. New monograph series devoted to Hellenistic themes were established in Italy and the United States, and they have continued to flourish to the present day. Hellenistic studies now

---

10 Quoting E. Olshausen, *Gnomon* 48 (1976) 461.

11 Stanley M. Burstein, "Hellenistic Culture Recent Resources (1960-1989)," *Choice* 27 (1990) 1634-1643. For more thematic surveys of Hellenistic scholarship see Frank W. Walbank, "The Hellenistic World: New Trends and Directions," *Scripta Classica Israelica* 11 (1991/92) 90-113; and "Recent work in Hellenistic History: Review Article," *Dialogus* 3 (1996) 111-119.

12 E.g. *Egitto e Storia Antica dall'Ellenismo all'Età Araba: Bilancio di un Confronto*, Lucia Criscuolo and Giovanni Geraci (edd), (Bologna 1989); *Hellenistic History and Culture*, Peter Green (ed), (Berkeley and Los Angeles 1993); *Images and Ideologies: Self-Definition in the Hellenistic World*, Anthony W. Bulloch *et al.*, (edd), (Berkeley and Los Angeles 1993); and *Alexandria and Alexandrianism* (Malibu CA 1996).

13 Seven volumes of the proceedings of the conferences held in connection with this project have appeared to date.

has its own APA interest group and even an e-mail discussion list.

The new Hellenistic historiography is not simply a continuation of the tradition that began with Droysen. Historians have changed fundamentally their perspective on the character and significance of the Hellenistic period itself. Starr observed (19) that, more than other period of ancient history, the Hellenistic period seems near to our own. Whether illusion or not, this sense of contemporaneity has characterized modern Hellenistic scholarship from its inception. But while the founders of Hellenistic historiography were inspired by the establishment of the modern European empires, contemporary scholars came to maturity in the age of decolonization. Not surprisingly, the dominant theme of recent Hellenistic scholarship is skepticism concerning their predecessors' optimistic picture of Greco-Macedonian invaders and their Near Eastern subjects harmoniously living together and cooperating in the creation of a brilliant new mixed civilization. So, in his brilliantly written *Alexander to Actium*—the premier volume of the University of California Press' successful Hellenistic Culture and Society Series—Peter Green[14] characterized the "whole notion of a conscious, idealistic, missionary propagation in conquered territories of Greek culture...as a pernicious myth...designed...to provide moral justification for what was, in essence, despite its romantic popularity, large scale economic and imperial exploitation." Because of the constraints of space, I can provide only a cursory survey of some of the achievements of this new scholarship. Like Starr, I will emphasize publications in English and defer treatment of recent scholarship bearing on Roman involvement in the eastern Mediterranean to the chapter on the Roman Republic.

## ALEXANDER THE GREAT

In the beginning was Alexander. Since Droysen, Alexander has been the central figure in Hellenistic historiography, and nowhere has the contemporary revisionist trend had more dramatic effect. For much of the twentieth century scholarship was dominated by a benign view of Alexander that reached its climax in W. W. Tarn's famous 1948 biography. This tradition continues to have a vigorous champion in N. G. L. Hammond,

---

[14] Peter Green, *Alexander to Actium: The Historical Evolution of the Hellenistic Age* (Berkeley and Los Angeles 1990) xv.

whose most recent work, *The Genius of Alexander the Great*, portrays the king as a "visionary statesman and general, the force behind a kingdom which rose above racism and nationalism to enjoy peace and prosperity."[15] But already in the 1980s, when Starr wrote, such idealistic assessments of Alexander had become rare, and Hammond is now almost alone in his espousal of them.

The decisive critique of such idealized interpretations of Alexander had been made almost two decades earlier by E. Badian, who conclusively established in an important series of articles the apologetic character of the "official" tradition represented by Arrian's *Anabasis Alexandri* that underpinned idealistic biographies such as those of Tarn and Hammond. In its place Badian[16] offered a deliberately "tough minded" view of Alexander as a ruler who brooked no opposition in his drive to achieve personal autocracy and glory through conquest. Badian's "ruthless Realpolitiker," in Starr's phrase (20), still retained, however, some traces of the mystique that had enveloped the more positive Alexanders of his predecessors. Not so the Alexander's of the 1990s!

Badian's critique of Arrian and his sources inevitably led to the rehabilitation of the negative tradition concerning Alexander found in the "vulgate" sources. The result is evident in the recent studies of John Maxwell O'Brien and A. B. Bosworth. Combining the "vulgate" with modern medical theory, O'Brien[17] diagnosed the Macedonian king as a classic alcoholic in one of the most unusual biographies of Alexander ever written. Bosworth, on the other hand, after producing in the 1980s a masterful study of Alexander as an efficient but ruthless conqueror in *Conquest and Empire: The Reign of Alexander the Great*,[18] has conjured up in his most recent work, *Alexander and the East*, a grim vision of Alexander as primarily a butcher, who "spent much of his time killing and directing killing, and,

---

[15] N. G. L. Hammond, *The Genius of Alexander the Great* (Chapel Hill 1997). The quotation is from the University of North Carolina Press advertisement.

[16] Badian, unfortunately, has never produced a general study of Alexander. His views emerge most clearly in E. Badian, "Alexander the Great and the Loneliness of Power," *Studies in Greek and Roman History* (Oxford 1964) 192-205; and "Alexander in Iran," *The Cambridge History of Iran* 2 (Cambridge 1985) 420-501.

[17] John Maxwell O'Brien, *Alexander the Great: The Invisible Enemy* (London 1992).

[18] A. B. Bosworth, *Conquest and Empire: The Reign of Alexander the Great* (Cambridge 1988).

arguably, killing was what he did best."[19] Far from being the creator of a new world, Alexander has become in the new Hellenistic historiography primarily the destroyer of the old world of the Persian empire.

In these circumstances, it is understandable that some of the most positive works of the past decade have concerned not the history of Alexander himself but the history of his image in antiquity. Pride of place belongs to two works: *Faces of Power*, Andrew Stewart's[20] magisterial study of the iconography of Alexander and its relationship to developments in Hellenistic politics and culture; and *The Coinage in the Name of Alexander the Great and Philip Arrhidaeus: A British Museum Catalogue*, Martin J. Price's[21] comprehensive catalogue of the enormous lifetime and posthumous Alexander coinages. Alexander's literary image has not been ignored, although no comparable synthesis has yet appeared. A. B. Bosworth has, however, provided in *Alexander and the East: The Tragedy of Triumph* an illuminating analysis of the ancient accounts of Alexander's eastern campaign. The extant ancient biographies also have received renewed attention. Both A. B. Bosworth[22] and J. E. Atkinson[23] have continued their invaluable commentaries on Arrian's *Anabasis Alexandri* and Curtius Rufus' *Historiae*, while Bosworth[24] has also produced an important revisionist intellectual biography of Arrian that tries to situate the *Anabasis Alexandri* in the context of Hadrianic instead of Antonine Rome. Waldemar Heckel has produced a new translation and detailed commentary on Justin's Alexander books[25] while N. G.

[19] A. B. Bosworth, *Alexander and the East: The Tragedy of Triumph* (Oxford 1996) v.

[20] Andrew Stewart, *Faces of Power: Alexander's Image and Hellenistic Politics* (Berkeley and Los Angeles 1993).

[21] Martin Jessop Price, *The Coinage in the Name of Alexander the Great and Philip Arrhidaeus: A British Museum Catalogue*, 2 vols. (Zurich and London 1991).

[22] A. B. Bosworth, *A Historical Commentary on Arrian's History of Alexander, II* (Oxford 1995).

[23] J. E. Atkinson, *A Commentary on Q. Curtius Rufus' Historiae Alexandri Magni, Books 5 to 7.2, Acta Classica* Supplementum 1 (Amsterdam 1994).

[24] A. B. Bosworth, *From Arrian to Alexander: Studies in Historical Interpretation* (Oxford 1988).

[25] Waldemar Heckel and John Yardley, trans. and comm., *Justin's Epitome of the Philippic History of Pompeius Trogus, Vol. 1: Books 11-12, Alexander the Great* (Oxford 1997).

L. Hammond[26] has extended his meticulous study of the sources of the vulgate tradition on Alexander to include Plutarch.

One of the most potentially fruitful developments of the past decade has been the renewal of scholarly interest in the importance of the *Alexander Romance* for understanding the Hellenistic popular tradition concerning Alexander. Behind this new interest in the historiographic significance of the *Alexander Romance* is a series of papyrological and epigraphic discoveries[27] that makes it increasingly likely that the core of that bizarre work is Hellenistic. Numerous puzzles remain unsolved, but Peter Fraser[28] and Waldemar Heckel[29] have made a good start on their solution with studies of possible political contexts for two of the *Romance's* principal sources, the list of Alexander's purported city foundations and the *Liber de Morte Testamentumque Alexandri Magni*. Another consequence of the deconstruction of the image of Alexander as creator of the Hellenistic world has been renewed interest in his successors and their achievements.

## THE DIADOCHOI

Starr ignored the Diadochoi in his survey of Hellenistic historiography. He had good reason for this, at first glance startling, omission. Prior to the late 1980s, only three books concerning Alexander's successors had been published in English during the twentieth century: C. A. Kincaid's[30] superficial popular survey, *The Successors of Alexander the Great*, E. T. Newell's monograph on *The Coinages of Demetrius Poliorcetes*,[31] and Mary Renault's[32] fascinating novel *Funeral Games*. The drought of scholarly studies of the Diadochoi has now ended. Indeed, works on the Diadochoi have proliferated since 1987. Full scale biographies of Antigonus the

---

[26] N. G. L. Hammond, *Sources for Alexander the Great* (Cambridge 1993).

[27] The most recent is the identification of a quotation from one of the letters of Darius on a first century A.D. *Tabula Iliaca* in the Getty Collection (Stanley M. Burstein, "*SEG* 33.802 and the Alexander Romance," *ZPE* 77 [1989] 275-276).

[28] P. M. Fraser, *Cities of Alexander the Great* (Oxford 1996).

[29] Waldemar Heckel, *The Last Days and Testament of Alexander the Great: A Prosopographic Study*, *Historia* Einzelschriften 56 (Stuttgart 1988).

[30] C. A. Kincaid, *The Successors of Alexander the Great* (London 1930).

[31] Edward T. Newell, *The Coinages of Demetrius Poliorcetes* (Chicago n.d.).

[32] Mary Renault, *Funeral Games* (New York 1981).

One-Eyed,[33] Ptolemy I,[34] and Seleucus[35] have appeared and, *mirabile dictu*, no less than three of Lysimachus.[36]

Work on the Diadochoi has not been limited to biographies. Waldemar Heckel's invaluable *The Marshals of Alexander's Empire*,[37] which finally replaces Helmut Berve's *Das Alexanderreich* for the figures it treats, has illuminated the milieu from which the Diadochoi emerged. Richard Billows[38] and Getzel Cohen[39] clarified the full extent and significance of the colonizing activities of the Diadochoi in Europe and Anatolia and the complexity of their relations with the Greeks. John D. Grainger[40] performed a similar service for the Near East by documenting the important contribution of Seleucus I and Antiochus I to the reurbanization of Syria. Finally, following the lead of Louis Robert, Richard Billows also deepened our understanding of the complexity of the age of the Diadochoi by reconstructing the fragmentary history of the various Macedonian and non-Macedonian dynasts who proliferated in Hellenistic Anatolia.[41] Two themes dominate all these works: the Diadochoi and not Alexander were the true founders of the Hellenistic state system and their creations were rooted in Macedonian tradition.

## MACEDON AND GREECE

Alone of the Hellenistic kingdoms, Antigonid Macedon is blessed with a relative abundance of literary sources, a situation that has encouraged a historiography dominated by narrative histories such as N. G. L. Hammond's monumental three

---

[33] Richard A. Billows, *Antigonos the One-Eyed and the Creation of the Hellenistic State* (Berkeley and Los Angeles 1990).

[34] Walter M. Ellis, *Ptolemy of Egypt* (London 1994).

[35] John D. Grainger, *Seleukos Nikator: Constructing a Hellenistic Kingdom* (London 1990).

[36] Helen S. Lund, *Lysimachus: A Study in Early Hellenistic Kingship* (London 1992); F. Landucci Gattinoni, *Lisimaco di Tracia. Un sovrano nella prospettiva del primo ellenismo* (Milan 1992); and Carlo Franco, *Il Regno di Lisimaco: Strutture Amministrative e Rapporti con le Citta* (Pisa 1993).

[37] Waldemar Heckel, *The Marshals of Alexander's Empire* (London 1992).

[38] Richard A. Billows, *Kings and Colonists: Aspects of Macedonian Imperialism*, *Columbia Studies in the Classical Tradition* 22 (Leiden 1995).

[39] Getzel M. Cohen, *The Hellenistic Settlements in Europe, the Islands, and Asia Minor* (Berkeley and Los Angeles 1995).

[40] John D. Grainger, *The Cities of Seleukid Syria* (Oxford 1990).

[41] Billows, (n.38), 81-109.

volume *A History of Macedonia* and biographies of various Macedonian kings.[42] At the same time, however, Macedonian historiography has been distorted by the Greek and Roman biases of the extant sources, which have diverted the attention of scholars from the internal history of Macedon to the study of Macedonian foreign relations, especially Macedonian relations with Greece and Rome. Starr (25) already noted tentative efforts by Harry Dell and others to compensate for the Greco-Roman bias of Macedonian historiography by teasing out of the sources data on Macedon's northern and western frontiers. Still, while these studies broadened the perspective of Macedonian historiography, the confusion of the history of Macedonian foreign policy with the history of Macedon remained largely unchanged. Only in constitutional history was there a move toward a more Macedonian centered historiography with Malcolm Errington's successful deconstruction of the notion of a Macedonian *Staatsrecht* in which the Macedonian monarchy was limited by the "traditional" rights of the Macedonian people,[43] and Elizabeth Carney's[44] demonstration of the significant role played by queens in the functioning of the Macedonian monarchy.

This situation has begun to change. The remarkable expansion of Macedonian archaeology since the 1970s has made possible for the first time the creation of a true Macedonian centered historiography. Eugene Borza has given us a model of what an archaeologically based history of pre-Hellenistic Macedonia would be like in his *In the Shadow of Olympus*.[45] Thanks to the work of the Greek Antiquities Service and the Research Center for Greek and Roman Antiquity of the National Hellenic Research Foundation, the archaeological and

---

[42] A new biography of Antigonus Gonatas has just appeared: Janice Gabbert, *Antigonus II Gonatas: A Political Biography* (London 1997).

[43] Errington's views are conveniently summed up in R. Malcolm Errington, *A History of Macedonia*, trans. by Catherine Errington (Berkeley and Los Angeles 1990).

[44] Carney has developed her ideas in numerous articles published during the past two decades. Her mature views are most conveniently accessible in Elizabeth Carney, "Women and *Basileia*: Legitimacy and Female Political Action in Macedonia," *CJ* 90 (1995) 367-391.

[45] Eugene N. Borza, *In the Shadow of Olympus: The Emergence of Macedon* (Princeton 1990). Borza's most important articles on Macedonian history are conveniently collected in *MAKEDONIKA: Essays by Eugene N. Borza*, edited by Carol G. Thomas (Claremont 1995).

epigraphic evidence for Hellenistic Macedonia also has expanded enormously during in past two decades. Although the public's attention understandably has focused on the controversy surrounding the identity of the individuals buried in the second of the remarkable royal tombs at Vergina discovered by Manolis Andronikos in 1977,[46] the new discoveries ultimately will affect our understanding of the whole of Hellenistic Macedonian history. Exploitation of this new evidence is just beginning, but a valuable synthesis of the new epigraphic evidence for the organization of Antigonid Macedon has just been published by M. B. Hatzopoulos, the director of the Research Center for Greek and Roman Antiquity. Despite the unprecedented expansion of our knowledge of Hellenistic Macedon, one fact, however, remains unchanged. The history of Macedon and the history of Greece were and are inextricably intertwined, so that it is appropriate to consider at this point recent work dealing with Hellenistic Greece.

Sixty years ago A.W. Gomme[47] protested against the view that the history of the *polis* ended with the battle of Chaeronea. The view against which Gomme protested still has its supporters. An important recent collection of essays on the classical Greek city concludes with an article entitled "Doomed to Extinction: The Polis as an Evolutionary Dead End"[48] Such views are not, however, typical of most scholarship produced in the last decade. Gomme's fundamental insight that the end of the political significance of the Greek city-states was not the end of their history clearly underlies most recent studies. As usual, Athens has received the lion's share of attention, and two achievements stand out: the successful conclusion of Christian Habicht's two decade long effort to provide an up-to-date political history of Athens to replace W. S. Ferguson's classic

---

[46] The most comprehensive publication of the finds is Manolis Andronicos [*sic*], *Vergina: The Royal Tombs* (Athens 1984). The initial identification of the burials in Tomb II as those of Philip II and Cleopatra is gradually yielding to one with Philip III and Eurydice (cf. the proceedings of a special session devoted to the Vergina tombs held at the 1990 meeting of Archaeological Institute of America in San Francisco and published in *The Ancient World* 22 [1991] 3-40).

[47] A. W. Gomme, "The End of the City State," *Essays in Greek History and Literature* (Oxford 1937) 204-248.

[48] W. G. Runciman, "Doomed to Extinction: The Polis as an Evolutionary Dead-End," in Oswyn Murray and Simon Price (edd), *The Greek City: From Homer to Alexander* (Oxford 1990) 347-367.

*Hellenistic Athens* [49] and Stephen Tracy's[50] bringing order out of the chaos of Hellenistic Attic epigraphy by identifying the styles of individual cutters and building dossiers of their surviving inscriptions. On a more somber note, Raphael Sealey[51] has provided a convincing but melancholy analysis of the inevitability of Athens' defeat in its struggle with Macedon in *Demosthenes and his Time: A Study in Defeat.*

Scholarship has not ignored the rest of Greece. New histories have appeared or are in press of Hellenistic Sparta,[52] Delos,[53] and the Aitolian League,[54] while the volumes of *Inschriften Griechischer Städte aus Kleinasien* continue their stately march across the shelves of our libraries. Particularly welcome is the recognition of one of the major achievements of the Hellenistic Greek cities, the widespread use of non-violent means—especially arbitration and *asylia*—to resolve disputes and limit violence; and the appearance of major studies devoted to these topics by Sheila L. Ager[55] and Kent Rigsby.[56] We especially need, however, further investigation of the new meaning of citizenship in Hellenistic Greece attested by innumerable inscriptions that encouraged members of the upper class to risk fortune and sometimes even life for the welfare of their *polis* and the reward of a decree of thanks passed by its assembly. Still awaiting full exploitation in that regard is the work of Paul Veyne[57] on the significance of *euergesia* in

---

[49] Christian Habicht, *Athen in Hellenistischer Zeit* (Munich 1994).

[50] Stephen V.Tracy, *Athenian Letter Cutters of 229 to 86 B.C.* (Berkeley and Los Angeles, 1990); *Athenian Democracy in Transition: Attic Letter Cutters of 340 to 290 B.C.* (Berkeley and Los Angeles 1995).

[51] Raphael Sealey, *Demosthenes and his Time: A Study in Defeat* (New York 1993).

[52] Paul Cartledge and Antony Spawforth, *Hellenistic and Roman Sparta: A Tale of Two Cities* (London 1989).

[53] Gary Reger, *Regionalism and Change in the Economy of Independent Delos* (Berkeley and Los Angeles 1994); and Nicholas K. Rauh, *The Sacred Bonds of Commerce: Religion, Economy, and Trade Society at Hellenistic Roman Delos, 166-87 B.C.* (Amsterdam 1993).

[54] Joseph B. Scholten, *The Politics of Plunder: Aitolians and their Koinon in the Early Hellenistic Era, 279-217 B.C.* (Berkeley and Los Angeles in press).

[55] Sheila A. Ager, *Interstate Arbitration in the Greek World, 337-90 B.C.* (Berkeley and Los Angeles 1997).

[56] Kent J. Rigsby, *Asylia: Territorial Inviolability in the Hellenistic World* (Berkeley and Los Angeles 1996).

[57] Paul Veyne, *Bread and Circuses: Historical Sociology and Political Pluralism,* trans. by Brian Pearce (London 1992) 70-200.

Hellenistic citizenship ideology. Be that as it may, as Starr
pointed out (24), Seleucid Asia and Ptolemaic Egypt and not
Macedon, were the great powers of the Hellenistic World.

## SELEUCID ASIA

Starr rightly observed (21) that of the all the successor
kingdoms the Seleucids rarely receive the attention they deserve
despite the fact that "their realm was the linchpin of the
Hellenistic World." Starr (21-22) also correctly identified the
reason for this neglect: the Roman and Jewish biases of our few
literary sources—Polybius, Appian, and *First and Second
Maccabees*—which encourage scholars to focus their attention
on the western frontiers of the Seleucid kingdom instead of on
its Mesopotamian and Iranian heartland. Works written in this
tradition continued to appear during the past decade. So, E.J.
Bickerman[58] traced the roots of Rabbinic Judaism to the
interaction between Judaism and Hellenism in Judaea in the
early Hellenistic Period in his posthumous *The Jews in the
Greek Age. Judas Maccabeus*, B. Bar Kochva's[59] massive
commentary on *First Maccabees,* illuminated the military
aspects of the Maccabee rebellion and much else besides, while
Doron Mendels[60] produced a perceptive study of the ideological
roots of the Hasmonean state. Nor has the rest of the Seleucid
west been neglected. John D. Grainger traced the rise and fall of
Seleucid rule in Syria and Phoenicia,[61] while a first step toward
updating David Magie's nearly half century old account of
Seleucid Anatolia has been taken with the publication of
Stephen Mitchell's monumental account of Hellenistic and
Roman Galatia, *Anatolia: Land, Men, and Gods in Asia
Minor.*[62] Finally, Anatolia: Richard Sullivan brought order to
the tangled history of the last years of Seleucid rule in the west

[58] Elias J. Bickerman, *The Jews in the Greek Age* (Cambridge MA 1988).

[59] Bezalel Bar-Kochva, *Judas Maccabaeus: The Jewish Struggle against the
Seleucids* (Cambridge 1989).

[60] Doron Mendels, *The Rise and Fall of Jewish Nationalism: Jewish and Christian
Ethnicity in Ancient Palestine* (New York 1992).

[61] John D. Grainger, *Hellenistic Phoenicia* (Oxford 1991); *The Cities of Seleukid
Syria* (*supra* n.40).

[62] Stephen Mitchell, *Anatolia: Land, Men, and Gods in Asia Minor*, 2 vols.
(Oxford 1993).

in his, unfortunately, posthumous *Near Eastern Royalty and Rome*.[63]

The Roman and Jewish biases of the literary sources for Seleucid history did more than divert scholarly attention to the margins of the Seleucid state. They also guaranteed that histories based on those sources would be histories of Seleucid failure. That such failure was not typical of the Seleucid kingdom as a whole is the thesis of what is surely the most provocative work in Hellenistic history published in the last decade, Susan Sherwin-White's and Amélie Kuhrt's revisionist study of the third and second century Seleucids, *From Samarkhand to Sardis: A new approach to the Seleucid Empire*.[64] Sherwin-White and Kuhrt maintain that, contrary to traditional opinion, the Seleucids assumed a still vital Achaemenid legacy and successfully maintained control of the core of the old Persian empire for over a century before succumbing to destabilizing forces set in motion by the Romans and the Parthians.

That *From Samarkhand to Sardis* has set a new agenda for study of the Seleucid kingdom is clear from the proceedings of a conference devoted to the issues raised by it that was held in Lyon in 1993.[65] Unfortunately, it will be difficult to carry out that agenda for the foreseeable future. Only archaeology can provide historians with the necessary evidence for a new history of the Seleucid kingdom, and bad luck has seemed always to dog the archaeology of Seleucid Asia. Most unfortunate is the case of Hellenistic Bactria, where the contemporary political chaos in Afghanistan has been accompanied by almost unimaginable damage to the archaeological record of eastern Iran. Politics have not, however, been the only problem. The premature deaths of Otto Morkholm[66] and Abraham Sachs have deprived scholars of the long needed replacement of E. T. Newell's obsolete studies of Seleucid coinage and the historical commentary required to unlock the historical implications of the

---

[63] Richard D. Sullivan, *Near Eastern Royalty and Rome, 100-30 BC* (Toronto 1990).

[64] Susan Sherwin-White and Amélie Kuhrt, *From Samarkhand to Sardis: A new approach to the Seleucid empire* (London 1993).

[65] The proceedings were published in *TOPOI*, 4/2 (1994) 431-610.

[66] The completed fragment of his projected study was published as Otto Morkholm, *Early Hellenistic Coinage: From the Accession of Alexander to the Peace of Apamea (336-188 B.C.)*, Edited by Philip Grierson and Ulla Westermark (Cambridge 1991).

Babylonian astronomical diaries so meticulously published by
Sachs and H. Hunger.[67] As a result, works such as Susan B.
Downey's[68] pioneering history of Hellenistic Mesopotamian
religious architecture, D. T. Potts'[69] archaeological history of
the Persian Gulf in antiquity and Frank Holt's[70] forthcoming
revisionist treatment of the kingdom of Bactria as a central
Asian state are likely to remain significant but, unfortunately,
isolated achievements.

## PTOLEMAIC EGYPT

Unlike Seleucid Asia, the abundance of evidence has
ensured that Ptolemaic Egypt has never lacked for scholarly
attention. The focus of that attention changed dramatically
during the past decade. The basis for that change was laid in the
1970s, when scholars recognized Ptolemaic Egypt as
constituting a distinct cultural entity with its own peculiar
characteristics instead of subsuming it in a hypothetical Greco-
Roman Egypt.[71] In the 1980s, social and cultural questions
began to supplant the political and administrative concerns that
hitherto had dominated the study of Ptolemaic Egypt and still
are reflected in Starr's comments. Particularly influential in
shaping the new scholarship was the work of the Belgian
scholar Claire Préaux who sketched out in *Le Monde
Hellénistique* a vision of social relations in Ptolemaic Egypt that
was surprisingly close to the fourth century B.C. Athenian
rhetorician Isocrates' dream of a conquered Asia in which
natives worked like Sparta's helots to support the new Greek
colonists and their Macedonian masters. In Préaux's view,
virtually separate Greek and Egyptian societies and cultures
tensely co-existed in Egypt with little or no interaction instead
of blending to form a new culture as earlier scholars had

---

[67] Abraham J. Sachs and Hermann Hunger, *Astronomical Diaries and Related
Texts from Babylonia*, 2 vols., Österreichische Akademie der Wissenschaften, Phil.-
Hist. Kl., Denkschriften 195 and 210 (Vienna 1988-1989).

[68] Susan B. Downey, *Hellenistic Religious Architecture: Alexander through the
Parthians* (Princeton 1988).

[69] D. T. Potts, *The Arabian Gulf in Antiquity*, 2 vols. (Oxford 1990).

[70] Frank Holt, *Thundering Zeus: The Making of Hellenistic Bactria* (to be
published by The University of California Press).

[71] Cf. the landmark article of Naphtali Lewis, "Greco-Roman Egypt: Fact or
Fiction?," *Proceedings of the Twelfth International Congress of Papyrology* (Toronto
1970) 3-14.

believed. Ethnicity was destiny and the ethnicities that determined privilege were Macedonian and Greek. Whatever Alexander's intentions may have been, Ptolemaic Egypt emerged in the work of Préaux and her followers as a society dominated by a tiny Greco-Macedonian elite.[72]

Evidence is not lacking to support Préaux's interpretation: obvious examples are prejudicial remarks about Egyptians in the sources, texts like the *Potter's Oracle* and repeated native rebellions. Nevertheless, the last decade has been marked by increasing doubts about its adequacy as a satisfactory description of Ptolemaic society.[73] The problems are threefold: first, it is based primarily on Greek textual evidence, which tends to ignore non-Greeks; second, it exaggerates barriers to contact between Greeks and non-Greeks in Ptolemaic Egypt; and third, like many studies of modern colonial societies, it exaggerates the extent of ethnic solidarity within the Egyptian population itself.

Part of the problem, of course, is that substantial social isolation characterized the one portion of the Egyptian population that is most visible in the Greek sources, the rural poor. Consideration of the social life of the Egyptian cities and the use of demotic sources suggest the need for a more nuanced interpretation. So, Dorothy Thompson's[74] brilliant study of Ptolemaic Memphis revealed a complex society in which "the interaction of two major groups of immigrant Greeks and native Egyptians...was of the greatest import". Likewise, the work of Janet Johnson[75] in the United States and Werner Huss[76] in

---

[72] The state of Ptolemaic historiography in the 1980s is lucidly surveyed in Alan E. Samuel, *The Shifting Sands of Interpretation: Interpretations of Ptolemaic Egypt* (Lanham MD 1989).

[73] The first sign of the split in scholarly opinion was the simultaneous publication in 1986 of two major synthetic treatments of Hellenistic Egypt, Naphtali Lewis' *Greeks in Ptolemaic Egypt* (Oxford 1986), which supported Préaux and Alan K. Bowman, *Egypt after the Pharaohs 332 BC-AD 642* (Berkeley and Los Angeles 1986), which was skeptical of her conclusions.

[74] Dorothy J. Thompson, *Memphis Under the Ptolemies* (Princeton 1988) 105. Cf. Janet H. Johnson (ed), *Life in a Multi-Cultural Society: Egypt from Cambyses to Constantine and Beyond* (Chicago 1992).

[75] Janet H. Johnson, "The Role of the Egyptian Priesthood in Ptolemaic Egypt," *Egyptological Studies in Honor of R. A. Parker*, by L. Lesko (ed), (Hanover 1986) 70-84.

Germany allows no doubt that the bulk of the Egyptian priestly elite not only prospered in Ptolemaic Egypt but, far from opposing the Ptolemies, were among the regime's strongest supporters. And not only the elite. In his elegant monograph, *The Ptolemaic Basilikos Grammateus*, John Oates[77] showed how one group of Egyptian officials, the royal scribes, exploited their possession of a critical skill, Greco-Egyptian bilingualism, to transform their "humble" office into one of considerable power and influence. In the private sphere Sarah B. Pomeroy[78] described how Greek women living in Egypt exploited Egyptian law for their own economic advantage. It is not surprising, therefore, that scholars increasingly view ethnicity in Ptolemaic Egypt as "situational" with individuals identifying themselves as Egyptians or Greeks depending on the circumstances and advantages to be gained[79] or that Demotists see the Hellenistic period as one of significant literary innovation and achievement.[80]

## CONCLUSION

Starr's essay was a perceptive but selective and personal assessment of the state of Hellenistic scholarship on the verge of an upsurge of scholarly interest and activity in Hellenistic history of remarkable breadth and richness. Inevitably not all areas of current scholarly interest could be covered. One particularly serious omission is Hellenistic historiography. The masters of that field in post-World War II America were T. S. Brown[81] and Lionel Pearson,[82] and Pearson[83] gave us a valuable

---

[76] Werner Huss, *Der Makedonische König und die Ägyptischen Priester: Studien zur Geschichte des Ptolemaiischen Ägypten, Historia Einzelschriften* 85 (Stuttgart 1994).

[77] John F. Oates, *The Ptolemaic Basilikos Grammateus, Bulletin of the American Society of Papyrologists,* Supplement 8 (Atlanta 1995).

[78] Sarah B. Pomeroy, *Women in Hellenistic Egypt: From Alexander to Cleopatra,* 2nd. ed. (New York 1990).

[79] Koen Goudriaan, *Ethnicity in Ptolemaic Egypt* (Amersterdam 1988); *Ethnicity in Hellenistic Egypt,* Per Bilde *et al.,* (edd), *Studies in Hellenistic Civilization,* vol. 3 (Aarhus 1992).

[80] Cf. the essays in *ACTA DEMOTICA: Acts of Fifth international Conference for Demotists, Pisa, 4th-8th September 1993, Egitto e Vicino Oriente,* 17 (1994).

[81] Most notably Truesdell S. Brown, *Onesicritus: A Study in Hellenistic Historiography* (Berkeley and Los Angeles 1949); and *Timaeus of Tauromenium* (Berkeley and Los Angeles 1958).

study of Timaeus' role in forming Greek views of pre-Roman Italy in his *The Greek Historians of the West*. Monographic studies have since appeared of Pseudo-Hecataeus' *On the Jews*,[84] and the *On the Erythraean Sea* of Agatharchides of Cnidus.[85] The most significant achievement of the past decade, however, has been to view the major extant Hellenistic historians as active participants in their own times and not merely as sources of historical data. A. M. Eckstein[86] has illuminated the moral views underlying Polybius' history of Roman expansion, and K. Sacks[87] and E. Gabba[88] have analyzed the contrasting attitudes of Diodorus and Dionysius of Halicarnassus to the turbulent events of late first century B.C. Rome.

As this necessarily cursory review of current Hellenistic scholarship indicates, the achievements of the decade since the publication of Starr's pamphlet have been considerable, and the future promises still more. So, the recent discovery of remains of the Ptolemaic royal quarter under Alexandria harbor is likely to change fundamentally our ideas about not only the city itself but also about the public image the Ptolemies projected to their subjects. Ironically, however, one effect of the remarkable progress in Hellenistic studies made during the past decade has been to highlight some of the field's deficiencies.

The most obvious and most frustrating is the fact that in the face of an enormous expansion in the evidence for Hellenistic history we still depend on research tools that are quite simply inadequate. One example must suffice to illustrate a serious and pervasive problem. Since 1913 the number of known instances of interstate arbitration has more than doubled from the eighty-

---

[82] Cf. especially, Lionel Pearson, *The Lost Histories of Alexander the Great* (London 1960).

[83] Lionel Pearson, *The Greek Historians of the West: Timaeus and His Predecessors* (Atlanta 1987).

[84] Bezalel Bar-Kochva, *Pseudo-Hecataeus, "On the Jews": Legitimizing the Jewish Diaspora* (Berkeley and Los Angeles 1996).

[85] Agatharchides of Cnidus, *On the Erythraean Sea*, (trans and ed), Stanley M. Burstein (London 1989).

[86] Arthur M. Eckstein, *Moral Vision in the Histories of Polybius* (Berkeley and Los Angeles 1995).

[87] Kenneth S. Sacks, *Diodorus Siculus and the First Century* (Princeton 1990).

[88] Emilio Gabba, *Dionysius and The History of Archaic Rome* (Berkeley and Los Angeles 1991).

two identified by M. N. Tod[89] to the 171 included by Sheila Ager in her magnificent new corpus. The work of Ager and that of Kent Rigsby on *Asylia* documents are, however, the exceptions rather than the rule. Said plainly, for the field to continue to develop and progress, much more effort needs to be devoted to completing works such as H. H. Schmitt's[90] invaluable collection of Hellenistic treaties and replacing venerable but woefully out-of-date works such as C. B. Welles' *Royal Correspondence in the Hellenistic Period*, L. Mitteis' and U. Wilcken's *Grundzüge und Chrestomathie der Papyruskunde*, and W. Dittenberger's *Orientis Graeci Inscriptiones Selectae*.

Equally or, perhaps, even more serious is a continuing conceptual weakness in our field. Ten years ago I remarked in a review of volume 7, part 1 of the new *Cambridge Ancient History*[91] that no satisfactory new general framework for Hellenistic history had appeared to replace the old "mixed civilization model". The situation still remains unchanged. Indeed, the most innovative scholarship of the last decade reflects that deficiency in that it emphasizes the regional and cultural diversity of the Hellenistic world instead of its commonalties.[92] Whether the trend toward the proliferation of regional specialties will continue or scholars ultimately will succeed in adumbrating a satisfactory new general interpretation of one of the most complex and creative epochs in ancient history still remains to be decided.

---

[89] Marcus Niebuhr Tod, *International Arbitration amongst the Greeks* (Oxford 1913).

[90] Hatto H. Schmitt, *Die Staatsverträge des Altertums*, Vol. 3, *Die Verträge der griechisch-römischen Welt von 338 bis 200 v. Chr.* (Munich 1969).

[91] Stanley M. Burstein, rev. of: *The Cambridge Ancient History*, Second Edition. Vol. 7, Part 1: *The Hellenistic World, Classical Philology* 82 (1987) 165-166.

[92] It is the central theme of one of the volumes in the Danish Council for the Humanities Studies in Hellenistic Civilization series, *Centre and Periphery in the Hellenistic World*, Per Bilde *et al.*, (edd), (Aarhus 1993).

# III

## THE ROMAN REPUBLIC

*Allen M. Ward*

In the ten years since the appearance of Chester Starr's *Past and Future in Ancient History*, which the present work celebrates and continues, there has been an amazing outpouring of scholarship in Roman history comparable to that in Greek and Hellenistic.[1] Old topics of investigation such as the origins of Rome have been fruitfully reworked, and topics such as women and the family, which were once peripheral, have matured into areas of central concern. In this new review of Roman Republican history, it seems best to look first at the current state and possible future directions of research on a number of topics according to the conventional periodization that underlay Starr's earlier discussion. Then, I shall look at some important areas of research that do not so easily fit into a chronological framework based primarily on political and military developments but that have received much more attention in both the scholarly literature and the classroom than they did ten years ago.

It is particularly fortunate that Professor Starr stretched his discussion of the Roman Republic to include early Italy and the period of Rome's origin. They form one of the most fascinating and dynamic areas of research in ancient history today. As he recognized, the standard books in the field at the time when he was writing presented views that needed to be superseded by syntheses based on the extensive amount of new research conducted by a new generation of scholars.[2]

---

[1] Chester G. Starr, *Past and Future in Ancient History. Publications of the Association of Ancient Historians I* (Lanham, New York, London 1987), hereafter referred to as *Past and Future*.

[2] *Past and Future*, 33 and n.2.

Much of that work has been and is continuing to be produced by an impressive cadre of Italian scholars who often provided the raw material for the masterly analyses of the late Arnaldo Momigliano. Ironically, when he died in 1987, he had recently finished his chapter, "The Origins of Rome," for the second edition of the *Cambridge Ancient History* and was in the process of editing volume I of the comprehensive *Storia di Roma,* which appeared in the following year.[3] In the latter will be found chapters by people like Carmine Ampolo, Filippo Coarelli, Giovani Colonna, Mauro Menichetti, Domenico Musti, and Mario Torelli, whose work has continued the process, already noted by Starr, of modifying the older picture of early Rome as being primarily agricultural and lagging behind the development of contemporary Greek *poleis*, with which it supposedly had little opportunity for contact.[4]

Indeed, a number of ancient authors saw early Rome as a Greek *polis*, and while that view cannot be accepted, enough evidence is coming to light to understand its origin.[5] Contact between Italy and the Greek world had been important during the Mycenaean Bronze Age, and while it was sporadic at best between roughly 1100 and 800 B.C., it had already increased significantly before the founding of the first Greek settlement in the West on the island of Pithecusae (Aenaria, Ischia) in the Bay of Naples during the mid-eighth century.[6] Probably early trade

---

[3] Arnaldo Momigliano, "The Origins of Rome," Chapter 3, *CAH*, ed. 2, VII.2, F. W. Walbank, A. E. Astin, M. W. Frederiksen, R. M. Ogilvie, and A. Drummond, (edd) (Cambridge 1989), 52-112; Arnaldo Momigliano and Aldo Schiavone, (edd), *Storia di Roma* I (Turin 1988).

[4] *Past and Future*, 34-36.

[5] Cf. Plut. *Cam. 22.2, Rom.* 2; Pompeius Festus, 326, 329 (Lindsay); Dion. Hal. *Ant. Rom.* 1.72-73; Ov. *Fast.* 4.64; Momigliano *CAH*, ed. 2, VII.2 (1989), 52-53 and 106-112. Massimo Pallottino has vigorously stressed the impact of Greek colonization on developments at Rome in *A History of Earliest Italy* (Ann Arbor 1991) and David Ridgway has echoed him in *The First Western Greeks* (Cambridge 1992). These two works plus Kathryn Lomas' *Rome and the Western Greeks 350 B.C.-A.D. 200* (London and New York 1993) help to fill a gap noted by Starr (*Past and Future,* 33, n.2).

[6] The evidence for the Bronze Age is conveniently summarized by David Ridgway, loc. cit., 3-10. Much more evidence, however, is needed before one can accept Emilio Peruzzi's argument for a major Mycenaean presence in Latium: *Mycenaeans in Early Latium = Incunabula Graeca* 75 (Rome 1980). Cf. Momigliano, *CAH*, ed. 2, VII.2 (1989), 54. For the important role of Sicily in the contact between the Eastern and Western Mediterranean during this period, see R. Ross Holloway, "Koine and Commerce in the Sicilian Bronze Age," *Mediterranean*

had already stimulated the formation of more sophisticated communities at or near earlier Villanovan sites associated with the emergence of the Etruscans in Etruria before the arrival of permanent Greek and Phoenician settlers on the shores of the Tyrrhenian Sea. By the time colonists had started to arrive in Sardinia, Italy, and Sicily after ca. 750, the Etruscans must already have been well enough organized to make it too difficult for outsiders to gain a foothold on their territories.[7]

The arrival of Euboean Greeks on the Bay of Naples—first at Pithecusae and then at Cumae—aided growth. Etruria, Latium, and Campania felt the impact of increased commerce with traders from the Eastern Mediterranean along the coast and up the rivers of Central Italy. Together they developed a Central Italian cultural *koinē* that included Greek and "Oriental" elements. Much of the evidence can now be found in recent works by R. Ross Holloway, Mario Torelli, and T. J. Cornell.[8] The orientalizing influences from Assyria, Phoenicia, and Egypt that appear in Central Italy during the early period make it clear that it is really necessary to be not just a Roman historian or historian of pre-Roman Italy but a Mediterranean historian to understand what was happening in Italy between 1000 and 600 B.C. Further discoveries will undoubtedly confirm and expand our understanding of the crucial role played by contact with the Greeks in the urbanization of the Central Italian coast in the eighth and seventh centuries, but much more careful work needs to be done to comprehend the mechanics and impact of the

*Historical Review* 5 (1990), 3-13. For the period between ca. 1100 and 800, see A. J. Graham, *CAH*, ed. 2, III.3 (1982), 95 and M. Torelli, "Il commercio greco in Etruria tra l'viii d. il vi secolo a. C.," *Il commercio Greco nel Tirreno in eta arcaica: Atti del seminario in memoria di Mario Napoli*, G. Colonna, (ed), (Salerno 1981), 67-82. Evidence for early Phoenician activity in the Tyrrhenian sea between 1000 B.C. and the establishment of permanent settlements in the eighth century has been found on Sardinia. See the articles by F. M. Cross and Ferruccio Barraca in *Studies in Sardinian Archaeology*, Volume II: *Sardinia in the Mediterranean*, Miriam Balmuth, (ed), (Ann Arbor 1986), 117-145.

[7] Annette Rathje, "Oriental Imports in Etruria in the Eighth and Seventh Centuries B.C.: Their origins and Implications," in *Italy before the Romans: The Iron Age, Orientalizing, and Etruscan Periods,* David and Franchesca R. Ridgway, (edd), (London, New York, San Francisco 1979), 179; C. J. Smith, *Early Rome and Latium: Economy and Society c. 1000 to 500 B.C.* (Oxford 1996), 72-77.

[8] R. Ross Holloway, *The Archaeology of Early Rome and Latium* (London and New York 1994); Mario Torelli, *CAH*, ed. 2, VII.2 (1989), 51; T. J. Cornell, *The Beginnings of Rome: Italy and Rome from the Bronze Age to the Punic Wars (c. 1,000-264 B.C.)* (London and New York 1995), 163-165.

"Oriental" contacts. As Momigliano said, "Phoenician contributions to the development of urban life in Central Italy must at least be treated as a serious possibility."[9] Right now, however, those who see Phoenician traders resident in Italy before the sixth century are supported by too little evidence.[10]

The unquestionable fact is that from the mid-eighth century onward, the occupied site of Rome evolved into a city within the context of the wider Mediterranean world. Greek imports appear in graves on the Esquiline Hill from 730 to 625, and one of the artifacts is a Corinthian vase inscribed with the Greek name Ktektos.[11] That is precisely the period during which Corinth and other Greek *poleis* were becoming physically and institutionally identifiable in Greece. One should not, however, conclude that the origin of Rome can be explained simply in terms of Greek or even Phoenician influences. Rather, it is more fruitful to see the origin of Rome as part of the same wider Mediterranean process that produced the archaic cities of Phoenicia, Greece, and Etruria. While looking for more evidence of specific contact with, and direct influences of, others on Rome is worthwhile, investigating parallels between Roman developments and those elsewhere will probably lead to greater historical understanding of what was happening at Rome.

A case in point is the whole vexed question of writing a narrative history of the Monarchy and Early Republic, which Starr, in contrast with his usual graciousness, characterized rather tartly as "...a saddening exhibition of largely fruitless labor," in which theories "are manufactured out of whole cloth to show the ingenuity of their creators...."[12] Happily, as he was writing these harsh but not unjustified remarks, the situation was changing despite the continued skepticism of Fergus Millar.[13] In a collection of papers on the so-called "Struggle of the Orders" in early Rome, Kurt Raaflaub called for a new comprehensive and comparative approach to the study of archaic Rome that characterizes the best work now being done.

---

[9] *CAH*, ed. 2, VII.2 (1989), 52.

[10] Ibid. and Holloway, n.8, 17 and 167. Cf. A. J. Graham, *CAH*, ed. 2 III.3 (1982) 95-101 and 186-87; J. N. Coldstream, "The Phoenicians of Ialysos," *Bulletin of the Institute for Classical Studies* 16 (1969), 1-8.

[11] Holloway, n.8, 22 and 167.

[12] *Past and Future*, 34.

[13] F. Millar, "Political Power in Mid-Republican Rome: Curia or Comitium?" *JRS* 79 (1989) 138-150.

By "comprehensive," he specified that "all available sources must be used adequately and to their full extent...not only the historiographical, epigraphic, and archaeological sources but also information scattered in the works of antiquarians and lexicographers, which is often hard to discover, and the evidence provided by linguistic analysis and social, political, military, religious and legal institutions."[14] The "comparative" aspect of Raaflaub's approach calls for seeing Rome in the much larger context of Italy and the Mediterranean world as a whole right from the earliest phase of its history. His approach champions the use of data from other times and places that are parallel enough with Rome despite being widely separated in time and/or space to yield probable and plausible insights supplementing what can be gleaned from limited or suspect Roman data. Of course, in situations where the Roman data are limited or suspect, the difficulty is precisely to judge what other times and places do provide real and, consequently, useful parallels. The comprehensive approach, therefore, is very important because it will maximize the amount of data available for helping to establish comparative parallels that will allow one to fit the data into more meaningful patterns.

Raaflaub was directing his remarks in part to a paper contributed by T. J. Cornell, who did not seem to pay enough attention to the deficiencies in the traditional literary accounts of early Roman history.[15] Cornell has taken Raaflaub's criticisms to heart in his subsequent work and produced one of the most stimulating studies of the Monarchy and early Republic in years.[16] For example, contrary to the long-accepted view, he argues that while Rome looked very much like Etruscan cities in the sixth century B.C., it did so not because it was under Etruscan domination but because they all shared in the Central Italian cultural *koinē*. The later shapers of the Roman tradition, he reasons, mistakenly deduced a period of Etruscan domination from the correctly-transmitted facts of late kings with Etruscan names and the similarity between what they

---

[14] K. A. Raaflaub, (ed), *Social Struggles in Archaic Rome: New Perspectives on the Conflict of the Orders* (Berkeley, Los Angeles, and London 1986), 9. Momigliano had already outlined such an approach in 1967 in a paper of which Raaflaub included an updated version in this same collection, 175-197. Raaflaub, however, gave a much more rigorous formulation of the approach, 1-51.

[15] T. J. Cornell, "The Value of the Literary Tradition Concerning Archaic Rome," ibid. 52-76.

[16] Cornell, n.8.

saw in Etruscan cities of their own day and the physical monuments that still survived from archaic Rome.[17] Instead of a hostile Etruscan takeover, a more likely explanation for the tyranny whose memory is preserved in the Roman historical tradition is the internal rise of tyrannical rulers along the lines of those appearing in contemporary Greek *poleis* like Corinth, whose social, economic, political, and cultural conditions were similar to Rome's. Accordingly, Cornell sees the last kings as populist tyrants whose attempts to restrict aristocratic power had prompted disgruntled aristocrats to take advantage of dynastic quarrels to abolish tyranny and seize control themselves.[18]

We have now arrived at the beginning of the Republic and the dreaded "Struggle of the Orders." Enormous amounts of ink have been spilt on these topics, but a consensus has emerged on some points and seems achievable on others. First of all, modern attempts to date the beginning of the Republic much later than the traditional date of 509 B.C. to some time in the second quarter of the fifth century have failed to gain wide acceptance, and there is now general agreement that the end of the sixth century is about right.[19] Although most scholars today would reject the simplistic picture of the "Struggle of the Orders" between rigid patrician and plebeian classes as depicted in the literary sources, they would agree that the terms "patrician" and "plebeian" are relevant to complex social and political conflicts in the first two centuries of the Republic.[20] Even the most radical recent critic, Richard Mitchell, who wants to abandon the term "Struggle of the Orders" and denies that "patricians" and "plebeians" have the historical meanings assigned to them in our anachronistic sources, does not deny that there were economic grievances and political conflicts within early Roman society.[21]

---

[17] Ibid. 151-172.

[18] Ibid. 143-150, 215-218, and 252.

[19] Raaflaub, n.14, 208; A. Drummond, *CAH*, ed. 2 VII.2 (1989), 173-178; Cornell, n.8, 218-239.

[20] Momigliano, n.14, 182 ff.; Drummond, *CAH*, ed. 2 VII.2 (1989), 182ff.; Cornell, n.8, 251-256; K. A. Raaflaub, "Politics and Society in Fifth-Century Rome," *Bilancio Critico su Roma Archaica fra Monarchia e Repubblica, Atti dei Convegni Lincei* 100 (Rome, 1993), 129-157 with a convenient bibliography in n.1.

[21] R. E. Mitchell, *Patricians and Plebeians: The Origin of the Roman State* (Ithaca and London 1990), 130ff. Mitchell's purpose, however, is not to describe those conflicts but to see how political and religious facts were misunderstood in the process of creating the picture presented in our sources.

Different theories about the meaning and validity of the term "patricians" are not very difficult to reconcile. The original patrician *gentes* probably were those clans whose members had the hereditary right to supply public priests called *patres*, who were also automatic members of the early senate. Since members of these prestigious *gentes* also dominated the curule offices of the Republic and obtained appointment to the senate, the term "patrician" probably had been extended at an early date to all of those who had held curule magistracies. No doubt, some wealthy, ambitious, and talented members of non-patrician *gentes* were occasionally able to rise to curule office and membership in the Senate through the patronage of patricians who were expanding their bases of support. They can be counted as members of the patriciate for all practical purposes even if they all did not succeed in establishing permanent patrician status for successive generations. In other words, during the early Republic, all *patres* and their *gentes* were patricians in the strict religious sense of the word, but politically the term patrician probably embraced all members of the governing elite.[22] That could easily account for the presence of certain names later identified as strictly plebeian in the early "consular" *fasti*.[23] If that were the case, then Mitchell is correct to argue that the notorious prohibition of intermarriage between *patres* and plebeians in the Law of the Twelve Tables is simply an attempt to guarantee that priests (*patres*) continued to meet traditional religious requirements, and attempts to endow the prohibition with the political purpose of denying plebeians access to the patrician aristocracy are otiose.[24]

Similar confusion has bedeviled defining the plebeians, the *plebs*. Scholars such as Raaflaub, Drummond, and Richard essentially view the original *plebs* as the non-aristocrats in general, whereas Momigliano limits them at the beginning of

---

[22] J.- C. Richard, "Patricians and Plebeians: The Origin of a Social Dichotomy," in Raaflaub, n.14, 122-124; Raaflaub, n.20, 142-148.

[23] So Cornell, n.8, 252-256. Cf. Raaflaub, n.14, 213-234 and Mitchell, who emphasizes the importance of curule office as the mark of an aristocrat, whatever name one wishes to give to the early Roman aristocrats, n.21, 22-35. The criteria for determining whether a *gens* is patrician or plebeian are not firmly established and in my opinion never can be. Cf. A. Drummond, *CAH,* ed. 2 VII.2 (1989), 175-176.

[24] Mitchell, loc. cit. 128-129. J. Linderski, supports the political purpose of the prohibition: J. Linderski, "Religious aspects of the Conflict of the Orders," Raaflaub, n.14, 260. In supporting the latter view, Cornell presents much evidence to undermine it, n.8, 255.

the Republic to those who were *infra classem*, those citizens who could not afford to serve as hoplites in the *classis*, the hoplite phalanx that along with the cavalry made up the *populus*, the formally organized army.[25] Surely, Momigliano was wrong to see the hoplite phalanx being composed mainly of the patricians and their clients, and he may go too far in insisting on a formal distinction that limited the use of the term *plebs* originally to only those *infra classem*.[26] In practice, however, it is probably right to identify the first "plebeian" protesters as the poorer citizens who served *infra classem* as light-armed troops. They likely felt economic hardships, deprivation, and concomitant legal disadvantages in the early years of the Republic more than those non-patricians who had the resources to serve as hoplites. It is possible, of course, that economic conditions were such that even some of the marginally qualified hoplites were suffering enough to protest.[27] Nevertheless, against Raaflaub's identification of the plebeians who staged the first anti-patrician protest as those who "dominated the phalanx,"[28] Cornell makes a telling point: "If the First Secession had been an uprising by the hoplite infantry, the conflict of the orders would not have lasted two days, let alone two centuries."[29]

---

[25] Raaflaub, n.20, 150; Drummond, *CAH*, ed. 2 VII.2 (1989), 166 and 207 f.; Richard, in Raaflaub, n.14, 114; and A. Momigliano, ibid., 182-185.

[26] Momigliano, ibid., 184-185. Even on the highest estimate of Rome's population at the beginning of the Republic it would not be plausible that the patricians and their clients composed the hoplite phalanx of the *classis*. Cf Raaflaub, ibid., 41-45 and A. Drummond, *CAH*, ed. 2, VII.2 (1989), 163-165.

[27] Cornell (n.8, 257) and J.-C. Richard (Raaflaub, n.14, 126-127) stress the impact of conditions on those who were *infra classem*. Drummond (CAH, ed. 2, VII.2, 235-238) gives equal emphasis to participation by those who qualified as hoplites and the light-armed infantry and also would include (rightly, I think) both urban and rural segments of the population. Cf. M. Torelli, "Dalle aristocrazie gentilizie alla nascita della plebe," *Storia di Roma* I (n.3), 257-261. Raaflaub accepts the widespread view that there was a serious general economic decline during the first half of the fifth century, n.20, 137-140 and n. 32 (useful bibliography). Drummond is more cautious, *CAH*, ed. 2, VII.2, 131-134, and Holloway is very sceptical, n.8, 171, but Cornell argues persuasively that the decline in fine imported pottery, in the quality of locally produced pieces, and in the evidence for significant building activity between ca. 474 and 400 B.C. in combination with the literary evidence for Rome's military difficulties in this period supports the picture of an economic crisis involving debt, shortages of food, and lack of land, n.8, 266. Cf. Raaflaub, loc. cit.

[28] Raaflaub, n.20, 150.

[29] Cornell, n.8, 257.

While an informal use of the word plebeian might well have included all non-patricians at the beginning of the Republic, those who initially protested in the name of the plebeians and tried to establish their own plebeian organization and officials were surely just a sub-set of the larger group whose interests they claimed to champion. Similarly, a modern "People's Party" is not made up of, and does not represent the views of, all or even a majority of those who constitute the "people" with whom the party seeks to be identified.

Raaflaub is doubtless right that at the beginning there was no large number of wealthy plebeians looking to become aristocrats who led the earliest protesters. Still, there must have been men with the time and resources to act as plebeian leaders; as he himself points out, the patricians had been relatively flexible and open in absorbing newcomers into their ranks and were not rigidly exclusionist at the start of the Republic.[30] Therefore, despite having many common characteristics, those who could be lumped together as patricians in early Rome must have had some differences in outlooks, aspirations, and agenda. Accordingly, just as some aristocrats in early archaic Greek city-states sought support from discontented groups against rival aristocrats, so some of the patricians in Rome would have seen opportunities for enhancing their positions on the basis of plebeian support.

Whatever the meaning of the prohibition of marriage between *patres* and plebeians, the patrician aristocrats undoubtedly defined themselves more exclusively as time went on in an attempt to monopolize the institutions of political power.[31] Eventually, however, they were gradually and grudgingly forced to yield to the pressures from below. That the social and political tensions did not result in renewed tyranny, reactionary oligarchy, or radical democracy in the fifth and fourth centuries is the result of the constant fear of attack by enemies bent on conquest (the same thing that kept the fragile American republic from self-destructing).[32]

---

[30] N.20, 144-145. Cf J.-C. Richard, in Raaflaub, n.14, 113-114.

[31] For the debate over the significance of the ban on marriages between *patres* and plebeians see above and n.24. For the gradual establishment of patrician exclusivity, see, Raaflaub, n.20, 145-147 and Cornell, n.8, 252-256.

[32] Cf K. Raaflaub, "Expansion und Machtbildung in Frühen Polis-System," *Staat und Staatlichkeit in der Frühen Römischen Republik*, Water Eder, (ed), (Stuttgart 1990), 538-539, and "Born to Be Wolves? Origins of Roman Imperialism," *Transition to Empire: Essays in Greco-Roman History, 360-146 B.C., in Honor of E.*

While the main outline of early social and political conflicts seems to be clarified, there are all kinds of smaller points that remain controversial and require more study. One such point is the size of the cavalry and hoplite *classis* at the beginning of the Republic. That seemingly small issue is linked with a perennial conundrum of early Republican history: the nature, names, and number of the major political offices between ca 500 and 367 B.C. Were there two chief magistrates, one for each of two legions, at the beginning of the Republic?[33] It is agreed that if there were two such magistrates, they certainly would not have been called consuls; however, there is little agreement on the proper term. Many different suggestions have been made: *praetores, magistri populi, dictatores, and iudices.*[34] If there were not two, then what do we do with the earlier consular *fasti*? How do we explain those pesky military tribunes with consular power from 444 to 367?

I suspect that at first there were only two major elected officials, a civil *iudex* who took over the civil functions of the old kings, and a *magister populi*, who was chief among the military officers, perhaps also known as the *praetor maximus*, who had the duty of driving the annual nail into the Temple of Capitoline Jupiter.[35] As for the Military Tribunes with Consular Power, Richard Mitchell may well be right that they were not connected with the schematized struggle of the orders presented in our sources.[36] Rather, they reflect the evolving state of the magistracies in the early Republic until the organization of the hierarchical course of offices (*cursus honorum*) that prevailed after the so-called Licinio-Sextian reforms of 367.[37]

---

*Badian*, Robert W. Wallace and Edward M. Harris, (edd), (Norman and London 1996), 290-292.

[33] Raaflaub has argued vigorously that Rome could not have fielded more than one legion at the beginning of the Republic, n.14, 41-45, while Cornell claims that Rome could field two legions, n.8, 189. This question requires a fundamental reevaluation. Current arguments all rest upon the demographic research of K. J. Beloch, *Die Bevölkerung der griechischen-römischen Welt* (Leipzig 1886), whose basic assumptions have recently been called into serious question, E. Lo Cascio, "The Size of the Roman Population: Beloch and the meaning of the Augustan Census Figures," *JRS* 84 (1994), 23-40.

[34] D. Musti, "Lotte sociali e storia delle magistrature," *Storia di Roma* I, n.3, 383-385; Cornell, n.8, 226-236; A. Drummond, *CAH*, ed.2, VII.2 (1989), 189.

[35] Cf Cornell, loc. cit.

[36] N.21, 139-142.

[37] Cf. Cornell, n.8, 338.

A much more interesting and fruitful topic of investigation has been the question of the creation of a nobility and its role in Roman politics and society after 367.[38] The Romans obviously meant something by the term *nobilis*, "notable," and generally understood who was a notable and who was not, but as is so often the case with words that everybody "knows," they never defined it. It has generally been accepted since Gelzer that a noble was someone who had held the consulship or was descended from a consul in his father's male line, but Peter Brunt has argued that patrician descent and holding or being related to a holder of any curule office also counted.[39] He may be right. Nevertheless, in the hierarchical world of Rome, the consulship, by virtue of its relative scarcity, its public prominence as the eponymous magistracy, and the conspicuous position of consulars in senatorial debate, always held pride of place. That can be seen from its receiving the highest place among the offices listed in epitaphs and from Cicero's enormous pride in reaching it as a "new man."[40]

After the priesthoods were opened to the plebeians in 300, becoming or being a consular *nobilis* was probably more important than being simply a patrician, and it was in the interests of either a patrician or plebeian leader to emphasize his consular ancestors in order to bathe in their reflected glory as he sought support for himself in reaching the coveted consulship. Recent studies have made it abundantly clear that the consulship was not the hereditary sinecure that it has often been made out

---

[38] Karl-Joachim Hölkeskamp has contributed three important studies: *Die Entstehung der Nobilitat: Studien zur sozialen und politischen Geschichte der römischen Republik in 4. Jhdt. v. Chr.* (Stuttgart 1987); "Die Entstehung der Nobilität und der Funktionswandel des Volkstribunats: die historische Bedeutung der Lex Hortensia de plebiscitis," *Archiv für Kulturgeschichte* 70 (1988), 271-312; and "Senat und Volkstribunat im frühen 3. Jh. v. Chr." in *Staat und Staatlichkeit* (n.32), 437-457. See also O. Wikander, *Senators and Equites v. Ancestral Pride and Genealogical Studies in Late Republican Rome, Opuscula Romana* 19 (1993).

[39] A. E. Astin has repeated the traditional view in *CAH*, ed. 2, VIII (1989), 169. Cf M. Gelzer, *Die Nobilität der römischen Republik* (Stuttgart 1912) = *Kleine Schriften* I (Wiesbaden 1962) and *The Roman Nobility* (Oxford 1969), a slightly revised translated version by R. Seager. P. A. Brunt, "Nobilitas and Novitas," *JRS* 72 (1982), 1-17.

[40] For two of the early epitaphs, see those of L. Cornelius Scipio Barbatus and his son ( *CIL* 1, ed. 2.6,7 and 8,9). Cicero was thanking the people right after his election (*Leg. Ag.* 2.3). For the importance of consulars in the working of the senate, see now M. Bonnefond-Coudry, *Le sénat de la république romaine, Bibliothèque des Ecoles française d Athènes et de Rome* 283 (1989).

to be, and clearly it was easier for a non-noble to get elected to lower offices because they were more numerous than consulships.[41] The point is, as Ernst Badian's recent study of the consuls from 179 to 49 BC reminds us, that to gain one of the only two annual consulships, noble ancestry was always a big help.[42]

Lately, three issues related to the rise of the patricio-plebeian consular nobility have generated much discussion. The first is the nature of aristocratic politics during the middle and late Republic; the second is whether the Republic was simply an oligarchy or whether, as Polybius claimed, there was an admixture of democracy in it; the third is the motives and practice of Roman imperialism both during the conquest of Italy and in subsequent overseas wars. Starr noted the main lines of debate on these three issues that were already hotly engaged ten years ago.[43]

On the nature of aristocratic politics during the middle and late Republic, Starr noted somewhat drolly,

> Since Münzer paved the way, recent treatments of the internal politics of Rome have been cast far too much in terms of factions, which are analyzed by prosopographical methods; but the popularity of chasing down who was whose uncle may at last be waning.[44]

Having myself been one of those who sometimes too zealously tracked down uncles—and aunts and cousins too!—I must be careful not to engage in what looks like special pleading. Since the death of Sir Ronald Syme in 1989, the consensus is that there were no stable factional alliances of noble families and their clients over generations or even a few

---

[41] Fergus Millar, "The Political Character of the Classical Roman Republic," *JRS* 74 (1984), 10-11 and *JRS* 79 (1989), 143. Cf. Keith Hopkins and G. P. Burton, "Political Succession in the Late Republic (249-50 B.C.)" in K. Hopkins, *Death and Renewal* (Cambridge 1983), 31-119; Jeremy Paterson, "Politics in the Late Republic," *Roman Political Life 90 B.C.-A.D. 69,* T. P. Wiseman, (ed), (Exeter 1985), 20-29.

[42] E. Badian, "The Consuls, 179-49 B.C.," *Chiron* 20 (1990), 371-413. For the importance of being part of an established family in the period from 366 to 167 see R. Develin, *The Practice of Politics at Rome 366-167 B.C., Collection Latomus* 188 (Brussels 1985), 96-102, and H. Flower, *Ancestor Masks and Political Power in Rome* (Oxford 1996).

[43] *Past and Future*, 38-45.

[44] Ibid., 41.

decades.[45] Still, I think that few would go so far as to support Robert Develin's statement that "the alternative to the relatively exciting faction fights of modern imaginations is a quietist and gentlemanly political process," which he prophetically admitted "the historian may find disturbing."[46] His conclusion is a good example of the bad things that happen when one looks only at statistics instead of seeing them in historical context.

Roman aristocrats lived in an intensely competitive environment that can be seen as early as the celebration of status in princely graves from seventh century B.C. Latium.[47] T. P. Wiseman has pointed out the similarly-competitive piling up of marks of status in a eulogy for L. Caecilius Metellus in the late third century, which have numerous parallels throughout the rest of Republican history.[48] If Roman aristocrats cut gentlemanly deals to ensure each other's election to the consulship, as the word *comparare* in Livy may indicate, they did so to cut out some other competitor.[49]

While long-term family factional alliances within the nobility must be rejected, the prosopographical approach to Republican politics still has its value. Particulars aside, at any given time, the Roman Republic was controlled by an oligarchy of prominent aristocrats, whether it was those defined as patricians in the early Republic or the more accessible patricio-plebeian nobility of the middle and late Republic. Politics were intensely personal and relied on dense networks of personal relationships. Male relatives might lend support to a man's career because his success would enhance their names too. As the hereditary patron of individuals and whole communities and one who controlled access to valuable resources an aristocrat

---

[45] T. P. Wiseman, "Competition and Co-operation," *Roman Political Life* (n.41), 3-19; J. Paterson, "Politics in the Late Republic" (ibid.), 21-43; E. S. Staveley, *CAH*, ed. 2, VII.2 (1989), 446 and A. E. Astin, *CAH*, ed. 2, VIII (1989), 167-174; H. Galsterer, "Syme's Roman Revolution after Fifty years," K. A. Raaflaub and Mark Toher, (edd), *Between Republic and Empire: Interpretations of Augustus and his Principate* (Berkeley, Los Angeles and Oxford 1990), 10-11; P. A. Brunt, *The Fall of the Roman Republic* (Oxford 1988), 351-502.

[46] Develin, n.42, 307.

[47] Holloway, n.8, 167-171.

[48] Wiseman, n.45, 3-19.

[49] For the practice indicated by the Latin word *comparare*, see Roberta Stewart, *Ritual and Legal Definitions of Political Power in Early Rome* [tentative title] (Ann Arbor forthcoming).

could count on the useful support of many.[50] Long-time friends could be called on and advantageous marital connections made. Therefore, aunts, uncles, cousins, in-laws, and old army comrades did matter. The problem is that we do not often have enough evidence to understand which particular ones mattered in which particular circumstances. Sometimes we do, however. At other times, we can at least can make a reasonable conjecture about who was part of a prominent aristocrat's network of supporters at a given point.

The abandonment of the factional view has led a number of scholars like Fergus Millar, Peter Brunt, Jeremy Paterson, Mary Beard, and Michael Crawford to de-emphasize the oligarchic control of Republican politics and put more emphasis on the role of the *comitia*, the popular assemblies, on whom the aristocratic leaders depended for election and the passage of legislation.[51] Ordinarily, the popular assemblies were dominated by landowners who shared the same outlook and values as the *nobiles* whom they regularly elected to high office and whose lead on legislation they usually followed.[52] Nevertheless, Rome's conquest of Italy and overseas expansion produced major social and economic changes that created serious differences of interest between large segments of the citizen body and the traditional political elite. That division encouraged ambitious political leaders increasingly to circumvent traditional oligarchic controls by taking advantage of popular elements in the Republic's "constitution" through appeals to the voters on popular issues.[53]

---

[50] Andrew Wallace-Hadrill, "Patronage in Roman Society from Republic to Empire," in A. Wallace-Hadrill, (ed), *Patronage in Ancient Society* (London and New York 1989), 63-87.

[51] F. Millar, n.13; P. A. Brunt, n.45, 19; J. Paterson, n.45, 27; M. Beard and M. Crawford, *Rome in the Late Republic* (London 1985), 51-52.

[52] T. J. Cornell, *CAH*, ed. 2, VII.2 (1989), 400-403 and E. S. Staveley, ibid., 443-455.

[53] A. E. Astin *CAH*, ed. 2, VIII (1989), 188-196. In a very salutary critique of too enthusiastic a use of the word democracy in the context of the Roman Republic, J. A. North has pointed out how aristocratic competition frequently determined the extent to which the popular will was voiced and how control of religion was a great instrument of aristocratic power: "Democratic Politics in Republican Rome," *Past and Present* 126 (1990) 3-21. One also should keep in mind how few Romans usually were able to vote, normally fewer than two per-cent in the estimate of Ramsay MacMullen, "How Many Romans Voted," *Athenaeum* 58 (1980), 454-457.

Of course, no governing class, group, or individual, however autocratic, can ignore serious popular grievances for ever and survive. Even if the aggrieved groups do not get a chance to vote, they can agitate, demonstrate, or riot and cause enough fear in those at the top to affect their actions. The Gracchi brothers and those aristocratic leaders labeled as *populares* are men who usually sought support from disaffected groups against competitors in return for helping to alleviate their grievances, a topic admirably explored by the Dutch scholar Paul Vanderbroeck.[54]

The Roman Republic's conquest of Italy and then much of the Mediterranean world took place in the context of both aristocratic competition within the oligarchy and popular pressure. Behind part of the early "Struggle of the Orders" lies the ever-present problem of land shortage faced by the peasants of ancient agrarian communities. War was the method often used to acquire more, and the successful leaders of such efforts were greatly rewarded with wealth and honor that translated into social and political advantage. The story of the conquest of Veii in 396 amply illustrates these points as the Romans destroyed the city, carried off moveable wealth, enslaved survivors, and divided the land amongst Roman citizens. In addition, the Romans faced intense and almost continuous threats from enemies bent on conquest which, in turn, shaped their communal and aggressive values.[55]

Cornell has rightly seen the conquest of Rome's former Latin allies in 338 as a crucial factor in Roman imperialism. At that point, Rome found the secret to her imperial success: the municipal system of Italy with local autonomy plus sharing the rights of Roman citizenship to one degree or another. Thus by sharing fruits of victory in return for helping to conquer the next enemy, the Roman elite kept their fellow citizens and allies happy with conquered land as they increased their own wealth and prestige through the successful deployment of ever-increasing amounts of manpower in war.[56]

---

[54] Paul J. J. Vanderbroeck, *Popular Leadership and Collective Behavior in the Late Roman Republic (ca. 80-50 B.C.)* (Amsterdam 1987). Cf. Jochen Bleicken, "Überlegungen zum Volkstribunat des Tiberius Sempromius Gracchus," *Historische Zeitschrift* 247 (1988), 265-293.

[55] In "Born to be Wolves," n.32, Raaflaub has admirably explored these interconnected topics and notes the important previous work on Roman imperialism during the Republic.

[56] Cornell, n.8, 364-368 and *CAH*, ed. 2, VII.2 (1989), 364-369.

The Romans' claim that they conquered out of self-defense is not always wrong, but their own economic needs and the driving ambition of a warrior ethos always ensured that they found a pretext to go to war when they were not given one by their next enemy.[57] That is why so soon as they had conquered Italy they started to conquer the rest of the Mediterranean. This conclusion has now been admirably reinforced by Valerie Warrior's careful analysis of Livy Book 31 and the outbreak of the Second Macedonian War, which set Rome irrevocably on the path to conquest in the East.[58]

The powerful role of the patron/client relationship that Ernst Badian had advocated and others denied in analyzing Roman imperialism has been defended with certain modifications in more recent scholarship.[59] Aside from the benefits that aristocratic leaders obtained through the exercise of patronage over foreign clients, the larger function of Roman patronage over foreigners, particularly in the developed East, was a convenient mechanism of hegemonial control without the bother of territorial acquisition. In a recent work on Roman imperialism in the East from 148 to 62 B.C., Robert Kallet-Marks has shown how after Sulla the senatorial aristocracy ultimately had to abandon the old hegemonial imposition of its *imperium* there in favor of the direct territorial rule that characterized the Empire. The key to the change was popular pressure created by economic motives, namely the need to secure Rome's food supply and a desire to maximize the wealth available to the Roman public.[60]

---

[57] Roman activity in Cisalpine Gaul between the first two Punic wars provides a good example. Cf. B. L. Twyman, "The Influence of the Northern Italian Frontier on Roman Imperialism," *The Ancient World* 23 (1992), 91-106.

[58] V. M. Warrior, *The Initiation of the Second Macedonian War, An Explication of Livy, Book 31* (Stuttgart 1996). One also needs to keep in mind, as A. M. Eckstein has reminded us, that many decisions in the wars of Rome's imperial expansion were taken by individual commanders in the field far from Rome and fellow senators: *Senate and General: Individual Decision-Making and Roman Foreign Relations, 264-194 B.C.* (Berkeley, Los Angeles and Oxford 1987).

[59] Peter Rich, "Patronage in Interstate Relations in the Roman Republic," A. Wallace Hadrill, (ed), *Patronage in Ancient Society,* n.50, 117-135; David Braund, "Function and Dysfunction: Personal Patronage and Roman Imperialism," ibid., 137-152.

[60] R. M. Kallet-Marx, *Hegemony to Empire, The Development of the Roman Imperium in the East from 148 to 62 B.C.* (Berkeley, Los Angeles and Oxford 1995). Much more interest has been shown in the acquisition of an empire under the

The pursuit of ever-widening conquests out of a combination of fear, desire for land, other economic benefits, and the competitive drive fostered by a warrior ethos produced the conditions that best explain the ultimate collapse of the Roman Republic. Peter Brunt's emphasis on the short-sighted behavior of the Republican aristocracy and its dominant nobles under the circumstances created by imperialism ought to be the framework within which all future discussion of the Republic's fall takes place.[61] Individuals like Pompey and Caesar had an important impact on events, but they were also the products of the political, cultural, social, and economic contexts in which they lived.

Some of the most important recent research in ancient history has focused on economic questions. Using archaeological as well as textual evidence and modern tools and theories of economic analysis has helped to produce a much more sophisticated understanding of such topics as trade, manufacturing, agriculture, and the economic role of ancient cities. The work of Moses Finley, Kevin Greene, Peter Garnsey, and Keith Hopkins has been particularly noteworthy.[62] Finley and Garnsey have followed the "primitivist/substantivist" school of thought, which held sway for many years with an economic model that portrayed the Roman and other ancient economies as underproductive and incapable of economic growth. Integral to this theory is the idea that the ancient city was a parasitic consumer that usurped the meager surplus of the countryside while giving back little in return.[63] Keith Hopkins, however, has shown the inadequacy of the "consumer city"

---

Republic than in its administration. Andrew Lintott has now remedied the situation in part I of his excellent book, *Imperium Romanum,* (London and New York 1993), and John Richardson has provided a useful summary in *CAH*, ed. 2, IX (1994), 564-598. Many more local studies need to be done, however, to elucidate the impact of Rome upon the provinces under the Republic.

[61] P. A. Brunt, n.45, 81-82. Cf. J. A. Crook, Andrew Lintott, and Elizabeth Rawson, *CAH*, ed. 2, IX (1994), 769-776.

[62] M. I. Finley, *The Ancient Economy* ed. 2. (London 1985); K. Greene, *The Archaeology of the Roman Economy* (London 1986); P. Garnsey, K. Hopkins, and C. R. Whittaker, (edd), *Trade in the Ancient Economy* (London 1985).

[63] Finley, loc. cit. Cf the discussion of Peter Garnsey and Richard Saller in *The Roman Empire: Economy, Society and Culture* (Berkeley and Los Angeles 1987), 48-49.

model for Rome in the late Republic and early Principate.[64] Using Roman Corinth as a case study, Donald Engels has forcefully argued for the "service city" as an alternative model to Finley's consumer city, and Neville Morley has recently done an extensive analysis of how the sheer size of the Roman market unleashed the forces of economic growth in the Italian hinterland between 200 B.C. and A.D. 200.[65] The methods and arguments used by Hopkins, Engels, and Morley have pointed the way for further productive research on the economy of Republican Rome and Italy.

Much good recent work has focused on the ethnic and cultural history of early Italy and Republican Rome. Starr's hope "that by now the Indo-European myth has been fully exploded both for Italy and for Greece" should be closer to realization for Italy at least.[66] Linguists are still quite properly trying to sort out the Indo-European languages and their relationships in Italy or with linguistic groups outside of Italy that might give some clue as to where some of Italy's pre-Roman population originated. Most scholars, however, seem to be avoiding the temptation to use this one cultural variable as a determinant of ethnicity and general cultural patterns that shaped the subsequent character of Latin-speaking Romans.[67]

The exception would be those who carelessly apply the work of Indo-Europeanists like Georges Dumézil and ahistorically try to read Roman social, political, and cultural history in terms of Indo-European archetypes. Dumézil himself

---

[64] Garnsey, Hopkins, and Whittacker, n.62, ix-xxv; Cf. P. Abrams and E. A. Wrigley, (edd), *Towns in Societies: Essays in History and Historical Sociology* (Cambridge 1978).

[65] D. Engels, *Roman Corinth: an Alternative Model for the Classical City* (Chicago 1990); "The Classical City Reconsidered" in R. Moorton and F. Titchener, (edd), *Mimesis* (Berkeley, Los Angeles, and Oxford 1997), 232-257. N. Morley, *Metropolis and Hinterland: The City of Rome and the Italian Economy 200 B.C. - A.D. 200* (Cambridge 1996). C. R. Whittaker has raised some important objections to Engels' arguments for the service city: "Do Theories of the Ancient City Matter?" in T. J. Cornell and K. Lomas, (edd), *Urban Society in Roman Italy* (New York 1995), 9-26. He does not, however, give enough weight to the impact of the monetization of the economy and the market forces that it helped to support. At least Rome and Italy seem to have become extensively monetized during the second century: K. W. Harl, *Coinage in the Roman Economy, 300 B.C. to A.D. 700* (Baltimore and London, 1996), 21-72.

[66] *Past and Future*, 33.

[67] E. T. Salmon, *CAH*, ed. 2, IV (1988), 676-719; J.H.W. Penny, ibid, 720-738.

realizes the historical limits of his Indo-European archetypes. For example, he believes that the functional triad on which he claims the social divisions of early Indo-European-speaking groups were based—sovereignty (which includes magical, sacred, and juridicial elements), physical power and bravery (particularly in war), and fertility and prosperity—were soon abandoned once migrating tribes settled and evolved into more complex societies.[68] Nevertheless, even he will argue that the original three Roman tribes, whose names are preserved in the historical tradition (the Ramnes, Luceres, and Titienses) originally represented functional divisions "with the Ramnes controlling political government and the cult..., the Luceres being specialists in war..., and the Titienses being defined by their wealth of sheep...."[69] At least, however, he would avoid the excesses of Frédéric Blaive, who applies to Sulla the Indo-European myth of the impious warrior who spends his life attacking the three functions although Sulla failed to fulfill all the requirements of the myth because he did not die a violent death.[70]

How dangerous it is to interpret even supposedly early Roman legends in terms of Indo-European archetypes has been brilliantly analyzed in T. P. Wiseman's recent book *Remus*. He demolishes the theory of the noted Indo-Europeanist Jaan Puhvel, who sees the legend of Remus' murder by his twin brother Romulus as being the Roman version of "the primordial sacrifice of the Indo-European cosmic twin."[71] Wiseman abandons the synchronic approach to Roman legends that Indo-Europeanists like Puhvel employ and makes a careful diachronic analysis of sixty-one recorded versions of Rome's founding. He concludes that the legend of Rome's founding by twins and the ultimate murder of the one called Remus evolved in response to specific historical circumstances and events between 342 and 266.[72] His hypothesis that legends like that of Romulus and Remus were often created for political and

---

[68] Georges Dumézil, *Archaic Roman Religion,* 2 vols., trans. Philip Krapp (Chicago and London 1970), 163.

[69] Ibid., 164.

[70] F. Blaive, "Sylla ou le guerrier impie inachevé," *Latomus* 47 (1988), 812-820.

[71] T. P. Wiseman, *Remus, A Roman Myth* (Cambridge 1995); J. Puhvel, *Comparative Mythology* (Baltimore 1987).

[72] Wiseman, loc. cit., 128.

propagandistic purposes through dramatic productions for a largely illiterate audience merits further investigation.[73]

That those dramatic performances all took place in the context of public religious festivals underscores the intimate connection between religion and public life that is known but too often forgotten by historians of the Roman Republic. Probably no one has done more to reveal the intricacies of Roman religion and public life than Jerzy Linderski, whose many meticulous articles are models of scholarship.[74] J. A. North, Mary Beard, George Szemler, and Roberta Steward have also made worthy contributions to the field.[75]

North and Beard have also tried to analyze Roman religion as a religious system radically different from those of the developed modern West. North stresses that whatever can be identified as Roman religion was a composite of different traditions—Latin, Greek, Etruscan, and Carthaginian—from the start.[76] Beard challenges the idea of a religious decline in the late Republic, although she sees significant changes taking place that differentiated it from earlier periods and caused consternation among contemporaries.[77]

An enormous amount of research over the last thirty years has greatly expanded our knowledge of public and private law under the Republic. Now has come a time of consolidation and synthesis. The most comprehensive treatment of law under the Republic is that of F. Wieacker.[78] The most convenient appears in the new edition of the *Cambridge Ancient History*.[79] Edward

---

[73] Ibid., 129-150. The whole question of literacy has been hotly debated since the publication of W. V. Harris' *Ancient Literacy* (Cambridge, MA and London 1989). He doubts that total adult literacy among Roman citizens before 100 B.C. was more than 10% (p. 329). See responses to Harris in Mary Beard *et al.*, *Literacy in the Roman World, Journal of Roman Archaeology*, suppl. ser. 3 (Ann Arbor 1991).

[74] J. Linderski, "The Augural Law," *ANRW* II.16.3 (1986), 2146-2312; "The Auspices and the Struggle of the Orders," *Staat und Staatlichkeit*, n.32, 34-48.

[75] J. A. North, *CAH*, ed. 2, VII.2 (1989), 573-624; Mary Beard *CAH*, ed. 2 IX (1994), 729-768; G. J. Szemler, *The Priests of the Roman Republic: A Study of Interactions between Priesthoods and Magistrates, Collection Latomus* 127 (1972) and "Priesthoods and Priestly Careers," *ANRW* II.16.3 (1986), 2314-2331; Roberta Stewart, n.49.

[76] North, loc. cit.

[77] Beard, loc. cit.

[78] F. Wieacker, *Römische Rechtsgeschichte I, Einleitung, Quellenkunde, Frühzeit und Republik: Handbuch der Altertumswissenschaft* x.3.1,1 (Munich 1988).

[79] Duncan Cloud, "The Constitution and Public Criminal Law," *CAH*, ed. 2, IX (1994), 491-530 and J. A. Crook, ibid., 531-563.

Champlin's recent study of Roman wills shows how useful legal evidence can be for elucidating Republican society and culture.[80]

Much excellent work is being done on the relationship between Republican intellectual and cultural life and its social, economic, and political context. Erich Gruen has written two stimulating series of essays on the reception of Greek culture in the Roman Republic and its relation to contemporary social and political concerns.[81] Another impressive example of this type of cultural history is the work of the late Elizabeth Rawson.[82] In a very interesting essay, Mauro Menichetti has traced the history of Rome's conquests in the architectural and artistic record.[83] More old fashioned but very useful works are Gian Biagio Conte's comprehensive history of Latin literature and Lawrence Richardson's replacement for Platner and Ashby's topographical dictionary.[84]

The most dynamic field of research in the last ten years has been that of social history. Previous preoccupation with the Republic's social and political elite has now been balanced by sophisticated modern studies of the lower classes.[85] The

---

[80] E. Champlin, *Final Judgments: Duty and Emotion in Roman Wills, 200 B.C. - A.D. 250* (Berkeley, Los Angeles and Oxford 1991).

[81] E. S. Gruen, *Studies in Greek Culture and Roman Policy* (Leiden 1990; paperback repr. Berkeley, Los Angeles and London 1996) and *Culture and National Identity in Republican Rome* (Ithaca 1992).

[82] E. Rawson, *Intellectual Life in the Late Roman Republic* (Baltimore 1985) and *Roman Culture and Society: The Collected Papers of Elizabeth Rawson* (Oxford 1991). See also M. Griffen and J. Barnes, *Philosophia Togata: Essays in Philosophy and Roman Society* (Oxford 1989) and M. Griffen,*CAH*, ed. 2, IX (1994), 689-728.

[83] M. Menichetti, *Storia di Roma* II A. Schiavone, (ed), (Turin 1990), 313-363.

[84] G. B. Conte, *Latin Literature: A History,* trans. J. B. Solodow (Baltimore and London 1994); L. Richardson, Jr., *A New Topographical Dictionary of Ancient Rome* (Baltimore and London 1992)

[85] Early examples are Z. Yavetz, "The Living Conditions of the Urban Plebs in Republican Rome," *Latomus* 17 (1956), 500-517 = R. Seager, (ed), *The Crisis of the Roman Republic* (Cambridge 1969), 162-179; P. A. Brunt, "The Roman Mob," *Past and Present* 35 (1966), 3-27 = M. I. Finley, (ed), *Studies in Ancient Society* (London 1974), 74-102; and Susan Treggiari, *Roman Freedmen during the Late Republic* (Oxford 1966). See now A. M. Burford, *Craftsmen in Greek and Roman Society* (London, 1972); S. R. Joshel, *Work, Identity, and Legal Status at Rome* (Norman 1992); J. K. Evans, "Plebs Rustica" *AJAH* 5 (1980) 19-47 and 134-173; P. Garnsey, (ed), *Non-Slave Labour in the Greco-Roman World* (Cambridge 1980); N. Purcell, *CAH*, ed. 2, IX (1994), 644-687; W. Nippel, *Public Order in Ancient Rome* (Cambridge 1995).

publication of Finley's *Slavery in Classical Antiquity* stimulated renewed awareness of the central role that slavery played in the social and economic life of Republican Rome.[86] One of the most innovative recent studies uses comparative evidence from modern slave societies to flesh out the less abundant ancient material and reconstruct the way in which Roman slaves experienced their servile condition.[87]

Black people did not have a major presence in the Roman Republic, but they were not unknown. Frank Snowden has assiduously collected all of the relevant textual and visual evidence and concluded that while Roman society could not be called racist, Blacks did suffer some color prejudice.[88] The problem is that the concept of race is irrelevant to Roman society. L. A. Thompson has used more social-scientific rigor in studying Roman perceptions of people of color. He points out that the Romans clearly distinguished between those labeled as *Aethiopes* and others who were *decolor* ("off white"), *fuscus* ("swarthy", "dusky"), *perustus* ("sun-bronzed") or *coloratus* ("browned") and that more than anything else, rank or class was a cause of prejudice.[89]

The most intensively studied social topics have been issues involving sexuality, gender, women, children, and the family. Inspired, as so many have been, by Michel Foucault, a number of scholars have explored Roman conceptions of sexuality and gender as cultural constructs and found that Roman ideas of male and female sexuality and homosexuality are quite different from modern concepts.[90] The social position of women, the

---

[86] M. I. Finley, (ed), *Slavery in Classical Antiquity* (Cambridge and New York 1960, repr. 1968). See P. A. Brunt, *Italian Manpower 225 B.C.-A.D. 14* (Oxford 1971); K. Hopkins, *Conquerors and Slaves* (Cambridge 1978); Alan Watson, *Roman Slave Law* (Baltimore 1987); T. E. J. Wiedeman, *Slavery: Greece and Rome* (Oxford 1987); Z. Yavetz, *Slaves and Slavery in Ancient Rome* (New Brunswick, NJ and London 1988); K. R. Bradley, *Slavery and Rebellion in the Roman world, 140 B.C.-70 B.C.* (Bloomington and Indianapolis, IN 1989).

[87] K. R. Bradley, *Slavery and Society at Rome* (Cambridge 1994).

[88] F. M. Snowden, *Blacks in Antiquity: Ethiopians in the Greco-Roman Experience* (Cambridge, MA 1970); "Iconographical Evidence on the Black Populations in Graeco-Roman Antiquity," in *The Image of the Black in Western Art*, I (New York 1976), 133-245 and 298-307; *Before Color Prejudice: The Ancient View of Blacks* (Cambridge, MA 1983).

[89] L. A. Thompson, *Romans and Blacks* (Norman and London 1989).

[90] E. Cantarella, *Bisexuality in the Ancient World* (New Haven and London 1992); A. Richlin, (ed), *Pornography and Representation in Greece and Rome* (New York

lives of children, and the nature of the Roman family have been the subjects of numerous books and articles.[91] Recently there has been an admirable attempt to integrate women fully into the general historical narrative rather than treat them as appendages.[92]

Two hotly debated issues involving the family have been the father's power as head of the family (*patria potestas*) and nature of the Roman family: should it be considered a nuclear or extended family? Richard Saller has rightly distinguished between the legal concept of *patria potestas* and the much less absolute power of the father in the actual workings of family life.[93] Much of the recent work on the Roman family has tended toward the view that it was basically a nuclear family. Andrew Wallace-Hadrill, however, in an innovative approach based on the study of Roman houses forces us to rethink the whole issue in favor of the "houseful" as a type that much more accurately describes the kind of family environment in which a large

---

1992); eadem, "Not before Homosexuality: The Materiality of the Cinaedus and the Roman Law against Love between Men," *Journal of the History of Sexuality* 5 (1993), 41-45; C. Edwards, *The Politics of Immorality in Ancient Rome* (Cambridge 1993). D. B. Konstan, *Friendship in the Classical World* (Cambridge 1997).

[91] S. B. Pomeroy, *Goddesses, Whores, Wives, and Slaves: Women in Classical Antiquity* (New York 1975) and "The Relationship of the Married Woman to Her Blood Relatives in Rome," *Ancient Society* 7 (1976) 215-227; J. P. Hallett, *Fathers and Daughters in Roman Society: Women and the Elite Family* (Princeton 1976); S. Treggiari, "Jobs for Women," *AJAH* 1 (1976), 76-104, "Lower Class Women in the Roman Economy," *Florilegium* 1 (1979), 65-79, *Roman Marriage: Iusti Coniuges from the Time of Cicero to the Time of Ulpian* (Oxford 1991); N. B. Kampen, *Image and Status: Roman Working Women in Ostia* (Berlin 1981); P. Culham, "Ten Years after Pomeroy: Studies in the Image and Reality of Women in Classical Antiquity," *Helios* 13 (1986), 9-30; J. F. Gardner, *Women in Roman Law and Society* (London and Sydney 1986); B. Rawson, (ed), *The Family in Ancient Rome* (London and Sydney 1986); S. Dixon, *The Roman Mother* (London and Sydney 1988) and *The Roman Family* (Baltimore 1992); K. R. Bradley, *Discovering the Roman Family* (New York and Oxford 1991); B. Rawson, (ed), *Marriage, Divorce, and Children in Ancient Rome* (Oxford 1991); J. K. Evans, *War, Women, and Children in Ancient Rome* (London and New York 1991); R. P. Saller, *Patriarchy, Property, and Death in the Roman Family* (Cambridge 1994); E. Fantham *et al. Women in the Classical World* (New York and Oxford 1994).

[92] R. A. Bauman, *Women and Politics in Ancient Rome* (London and New York 1992).

[93] R. P. Saller, "Patria Potestas and the Stereotype of the Roman Family," *Continuity and Change* 1 (1986), 7-22 and n.91, 102-132. Cf. Evans, n.91, 177-195.

percentage of the population lived.[94] His work reflects the increasing methodological awareness that characterizes the best research now being done in social history and that promises to enhance our understanding of Roman Republican society within the limits imposed by our highly fragmentary evidence.[95]

---

[94] A. Wallace-Hadrill, "Houses and Households: Sampling Pompeii and Herculaneum" in B. Rawson, (ed), (1991), n.91, 166-190.

[95] See T. G. Parkin, *Demography and Roman Society* (Baltimore 1992); S. Joshel, n.85, 3-24; and B. Rawson in R. Hawley and B. Levick, (edd), *Women in Antiquity: New Assessments* (London and New York 1995), 1-20 for useful methodological discussions.

# THE ROMAN EMPIRE

*Ramsay MacMullen*

Dr. Johnson paused to reflect on his production of an English dictionary, in three years, while it had taken the French Academy of forty members forty years to bring the same order to their language: "Let me see; forty times forty is sixteen hundred. As three to sixteen hundred, so is the proportion of an Englishman to a Frenchman." One may say something of the sort in tribute to Chester Starr, singlehandedly accomplishing what the four authors of this volume attempt in his shadow.

And the fourth and last part of our joint endeavor, covering the half-millennium and more of the Empire, might even occupy another four surveyors all of itself, not because there is a great deal more of it, geographically, than of any preceding period with a single focus or domination; not because it is longer, according to the conventional demarcation of periods by political form and legal system; not because the sheer number of words in surviving literary texts is vastly greater, to say nothing of the five- or ten-to-one ratio of its inscriptions, excavated sites, and various other archeological testimonia, compared to those of earlier eras. No, this abundance of evidence rather underlies and partly explains the chief reason. A much larger share of research energy has flowed into the Empire in recent decades, especially into its latter phases, attracted by the greater possibilities there: more questions that can be asked and answered, therefore more publication. From the early 1990s the disproportion could be quantified, at least in the western hemisphere:[1] nearly twice as many ancient historians by

---

[1] *AAH Newsletter* 62, Dec. 1993, 2. But the older view is still reflected in J. Boardman, *et al.*, *The Roman World* (Oxford 1988); devoting its first 400 pages to

profession declared themselves Roman, as Greek, and among the Roman, many times more devoted themselves to the Empire than to the Monarchy and Republic. Specialists in the late Empire (Diocletian to Justinian) approached a parity in numbers with those of the Empire pre-Diocletian. They even produced a journal, ultimate proof that they had arrived.[2]

What is to be done with this profusion, by way of general review? Shouldn't it be left to the very judicious list of titles compiled by C. M. Wells?[3] Or the familiar *Année philologique*, or Online Public Access Catalogues (OPACs, e.g. NOTIS) available nowadays on any campus?

Yet it was the ambition of Chester Starr to attempt something much more selective, and the approach he chose governs this present attempt also. Starting from 1980, then, I point out new methods and areas of research in particular favor or, if more traditional, then areas or topics wrapped up in some particularly admirable package, perhaps a magnum opus; and I emphasize what is in English—while confessing, of course, because I cannot control, the element of the arbitrary in my choices over-all.

At the start, a reminder: the ancient world may be fairly called a mature field of study. Its Clio is of a certain age. While still capable of a brisk step every now and again, she is most at her ease in a rocking chair, alternating, back and forth between novel interpretations and their correction through critical discussion. Her chair moves, indeed, but with a rather Brownian motion. Only truly new questions or facts can stimulate her into any noticeable advance.

Truly new questions worth asking are of the rarest; yet among specialists in antiquity as in other periods, everyone acknowledges a significant shift in interest from great men and their doings, to the not so great—even to women. Imagine! Once, political narrative dominated not only among the ancient historians themselves but among their descendants, and

---

that world only up through Marcus Aurelius, with an "Envoi" (401-422) by H. Chadwick on the rest, up to Chalcedon.

[2] *Antiquité tardive* (*Late Antiquitv=Spätantike*), from vol. 1 (1993).

[3] Three or four hundred titles on the Empire, each with précis, reaching back to favorites in the 1930s but mostly of recent decades, in *Guide to Historical Literature* of the American Historical Association, ed. 3, vol. 1 (New York 1995) 214ff. Notice also the bibliography in C. M. Wells' excellent *The Roman Empire*, ed. 2 (Cambridge 1994) (but, despite its title, the book covers only the first two thirds of the Principate).

application of epigraphic evidence favored the prosopography of senators and equestrians, back in the days of R. Syme. Certainly lower ranks received some attention, as they still do; but the emphasis was on how far they might rise in the world or how great their contribution was to the economy. It was something quite new to wonder how the lowest ranks related to each other.[4] To leave public life entirely and study the private sector required curiosity of a sort best satisfied by the school of the *Annales*; and the same school helped also to make more academically respectable and to deepen the study of sexuality and of the family.

As an illustration, take S. Treggiari's summing up of what is to be known about the institution of marriage among the Romans. Though the relevant law had been a hundred times examined, and writers on women in Roman antiquity had drawn their own conclusions, it remained to bring together both legal and non-legal sources, with results less clear (of course, that being the nature of reality) and far more believable. "Whatever her legal position, the wife with a big dowry was never really in her husband's control," so Treggiari discovers in poets and playwrights, in little mentions and anecdotes.[5] B. D. Shaw independently examines and lays emphasis on the degree to which law and custom may be expected to differ in marital relations and private life at large, today as in the Roman past.[6] Again, Treggiari notes what can be learned about women from the Vindolanda tablets, including our earliest autograph by a woman, Sulpicia Lepidina—to which, add the documents of Babatha discovered in a cave by the Dead Sea.[7] Babatha, born

---

[4] A good survey of problems, methods, and results of study in P. Lopez Barja de Quiroga, "Freedmen social mobility in Roman Italy," *Historia* 44 (1995) 326-48; but compare the greater alertness of M. Flory, "Where women precede men: factors influencing the order of names in Roman epitaphs," *CJ* 79 (1984) 216-224.

[5] *Roman Marriage. "Iusti Coniuges" from the Time of Cicero to the Time of Ulpian* (Oxford 1991) 329ff. (in Plautus, also Juvenal, "dowry buys them compliant husbands"); similarly on wives in business, 335, 379; and add L. Huchthausen, *Klio* 56 (1974) 199.

[6] Reviewing J. E. Grubbs, *Law and Family in Late Antiquity. The Emperor Constantine's Marriage Legislation* (Oxford 1995), in *Bryn Mawr Class. Rev.* 7 (1996) 511ff.

[7] Treggiari 422; the tablets over-all in R. Birley, *Vindolanda. A Roman Frontier Post on Hadrian's Wall*, (London 1977) 156ff.; A. K. Bowman and J. D. Thomas, "New writing-tablets from Vindolanda," *Britannia* 17 (1986) 299ff.; "Two letters from Vindolanda," *Britannia* 21 (1990) 33ff.; and Bowman alone, *Life and Letters on*

in the region under Nero, Jewess of Arabia and one of a Jew's
two wives (simultaneously!), herself illiterate but bilingual in
Greek and Aramaic, of some means, making a loan to her
husband and competent (through male representatives) to
litigate in the gubernatorial court when the principality became
a province—Babatha is even charged with violence in the
defense of her property. She is a reminder that women with
some force of character, provided they also had money, might
be expected to show up in our records as movers and shakers.

Out of the mass of papyri of the Roman period, focus on the
women of a single town, Oxyrhynchus, too, is useful because it
allows some sense of proportion or likelihood to appear. Here,
women can be seen as equal partners in the arranging of their
marriage contracts and, among hundreds of texts, acting to rent,
buy, or sell real estate or slaves; routinely lending money;
contractors to engage labor; and in all these regards, sometimes,
dispensing with a male spokesman. As might be said of
Babatha, so E. Kutzner exclaims about the Egyptian data, "It is
remarkable how many documents show women employing
force."[8] And looking to the west, in Ostia, there too it can be
seen how "women appear surprisingly often in inscriptions as
property owners."[9] Society made room for them.

The true assessment must thus be made through documents
not found in the Loeb Classical Library: "new" facts. Consider
the model for her sex in Seneca: "in the twelve years of her
husband's governorship of Egypt, she never appeared in public,
received no callers in her provincial property," and so forth.[10]
The passage underlines the contrast between public, political
power, by far the greater part in the hands of men even on the
local level, and other kinds wielded by their wives or widows

---

the Roman Frontier: Vindolanda, (London 1994). On Babatha, see N. Lewis, (ed),
*The Documents from the Bar Kokhba Period in the Cave of Letters, Greek Papyri*
(Jerusalem 1989); a summary by Goodman, "Babatha's story," *JRS* 81 (1991) 169ff.
Note the business role of another woman, Julia Crispina, in the same little archive,
representing herself in a law suit.

[8] *Untersuchungen zur Stellung der Frau im römischen Oxyrhynchus* (Frankfort
1989), e.g. 39, 82-98, and 107 (quoted).

[9] H. E. Herzig, "Frauen in Ostia. Ein Beitrag zur Sozialgeschichte der Hafenstadt,"
*Historia* 32 (1983) 78, with women independently active in business or as
patronesses and priestesses, etc.

[10] *Dial.* 12 (*ad Helv. matr.*) 19.6; compare another reality in Tac., *Ann.* 3.33, army
commanders' and officers' wives an element *ambitiosum, potestatis avidum...habere
ad manum centuriones.*

and their sisters in less prominent classes of society. It suggests, too, a contrast between what men praised women for—therefore what women's epitaphs will tell us (so much used for women's history)—and what anecdotes will tell. R. van Bremen,[11] in a very comprehensive and meticulous work, indeed a work of old-fashioned philological scholarship in the best sense of the term, emphasizes only the first as "power"; but Babatha and her like show how much more there was to it than that.

Within the area of private life, certainly the family as an object of study is most at home within the traditions of the *Annales*, witness its treatment foremost in French;[12] and when it is offered in the form of big encyclopedias, too, then obviously some period of discussion and laying of groundwork preceded. Nevertheless, it must still count as a new area—particularly in English; and within it, quantification offers a novel means of generalizing. Of this method, R. P. Saller and B. D. Shaw provide an especially good illustration.[13] Among their findings is the "heavy concentration on nuclear family relationships in funerary dedications at Rome [and] in every other civilian population of the western empire sufficiently influenced by Roman culture to erect funerary monuments," this fact running "counter to the traditional view based on legal concepts, which stresses the central position of the senior living male in the agnatic line.... The extended patriarchal family must have been uncommon." Particularly to be noticed here is the inventive application of non-literary evidence to questions previously approached only through more accessible sources, and the

---

[11] *The Limits of Participation* (Amsterdam 1996) 85, "influence", i.e., power, is dependent on "eponymous office"—therefore, no office, no power, in his view; and throughout (e.g. 202), he minimizes women's independence, while actually giving glimpses of something more, e.g., Menodora of Sillyon.

[12] A prominent indication in the project edited by P. Aries and G. Duby, *A History of Private Life*, with a chapter on the Empire in vol. 1, P. Veyne, (ed), trans. G. Goldhammer (Cambridge 1987); also *A History of Women in the West*, P. Schmitt Pantel, (ed), vol. 1, *From Ancient Goddesses to Christian Saints*, eadem, (ed), trans. A. Goldhammer (Cambridge 1992), where, however, there is not very much for the student of the Empire, except regarding women in the church (and ignoring figures like Lucilla of Carthage, whose impact on post-Pauline Christianity was much greater than that of most of the other figures who are included). Among more recent works in English, I mention only S. Dixon, *The Roman Family* (Baltimore 1992)—reader-friendly, the author widely read, describing herself (193) as "somewhat *annaliste*."

[13] "Tombstones and Roman family relations in the Principate: civilians, soldiers and slaves," *JRS* 74 (1984) 124ff., esp. 136 (quoted).

confirmation that reality did not correspond to formal, i.e. legal, structures. This, it may be said, is the lesson also of Babatha.

Private life as opposed to public—is that fit material for "history"? Is there nothing then that is *not* history? Suppose, as an absurdity, that one were to collect all that can be known about the occurrence, the popular perception and the everyday consequences of being lefthanded in the ancient world, and, for the sake of respectability, if one raised the subject to the level of academic jargon, as "sinisterity"—would that be generally seen as worth discussing? I think not. But why not? The answer has something to do with how much life was lived differently on account of whatever is the object of study: "no history" unless it can be shown to "influence events and social change."[14] A difference from antiquarianism does exist; the latter word and the distinction have a meaning we do understand almost without thinking about it. There can be no question, however, that research trends in recent decades have obscured the distinction and drawn the study of the empire away from what most people would call the center of interest. Where, in the past, the casually curious might have wondered at the answers supplied by specialists in the field, now they must wonder at the questions. A distance opens up between specialists (who may be undergraduate teachers as well as scholars) and the audience they may want to include.

The dimensions of that larger audience can be illustrated by a game, "SPQR," first appearing on the Internet, then on the Web, and available on a CD-ROM. Here Rome can be found as it looked under Septimius Severus in "a 3-D virtual world" with "flythroughs" of the city, a treasury of views, models, and plans of ancient sites and buildings, an illustrated prosopography, (invented) journals of representative individuals, and an *acta diurna* of the reign as it might then have appeared (sort of).[15] Many scores of thousands of persons have completed the many hours of interaction that the game offers, and scores of millions of "hits" have been registered on its web-site within the space of no more than a year. Such numbers, expressive not only of a liking for play but of curiosity in history as a story and with pictures, serve to quantify the general appetite for traditional historiography: for "SPQR" centers in public life and political

---

[14] I quote a conventional formulation by G. Duby and M. Perrot, in *History of Women,* (n.12), xv.

[15] My friend V. Rudich is my source, as well as the game's expert consultant.

narrative—specifically, in Plautianus' conspiracy and its implications for the empire as a whole. These numbers thus pull in one direction; new areas of interest and new questions pull in another. I think it right to take note of the tension even while, myself, favoring novelty over the traditional.

Traditional narrative accounts of reigns, even the briefest, continue to be written. Of Vitellius, for instance, one may find such a treatment as could not be easily improved on.[16] But it relies, because it has no choice but to rely, almost entirely on the ancient historians, a thousand times discussed. So, on this or that given event or motive or personality in Vitellius' life, Clio rocks one way where she not long ago rocked the other way, back and forth.

Consider three apparent exceptions: wonderful treatments of Roman emperors. And, first, that unique biography of Hadrian by a writer of fiction, M. Yourcenar, teaching historians their own game. Although written two generations ago, it is too good to pass by and should now be aligned with W. L. MacDonald's and J. L. Pinto's work on the villa.[17] To this latter work I return a little later.

Second, P. Zanker's study of the Augustan style, as it may be called: the messages and values projected to the public through all the arts, changing yet harmonious among themselves, giving rise to something fresh and pervasive and characteristic at the center of the empire. The author is insistently concerned with contemporaries' vision and their code of symbols and allusions. "A completely new pictorial vocabulary was created" in no more than the twenty years post-27 BC.[18] It reflected genuine enthusiasm and piety. Zanker's picture is a warm one, quite at odds with that calculating and dessiccated Augustus and his regime that once reflected merely academic reconstruction. Even naivety may be attributed to this first emperor; sincerity, to his upper classes and the not-so-

---

[16] B. Richter, *Vitellius. Ein Zerrbild der Geschichtsschreibung. Untersuchungen zum Prinzipat des A. Vitellius* (Frankfurt 1992).

[17] *Memoirs of Hadrian*, trans. G. Frick (New York 1990; first, in 1954). Syme devoted a long essay to correcting its mistakes (*Roman Papers*, A. R. Birley, (ed), [Oxford 1991] vol. 6, 162-80); MacDonald and Pinto, *Hadrian's Villa and Its Legacy* (New Haven 1995).

[18] P. Zanker, *The Powers of Images in the Age of Augustus*, trans. A. Shapiro (Ann Arbor 1988; German, 1987, of lectures of 1983-84); quoted, 101; "naivety", 102ff.; Porticus Liviae, 137ff.; and "The private sphere" in chap. 7, quoted, *re* a clay lamp.

upper, too, as they welcomed the age into their private homes; and awe, to the slum population huddled in their tenements around the gigantically elegant Porticus Liviae. Furthermore, and important to reflect on: "When the average man in the street bought himself a clay lamp with an image of the *corona civica*, Victoria on the globe, the *clipeus virtutis* or Aeneas fleeing from Troy, instead of one with a chariot race or an erotic scene, he was making a deliberate choice." By such statements Zanker leads his readers into the "why," the realm of motive and therefore of explanation, "affective" history (it may be called) beyond the "what." He is able to do this because the "what" has been so well chosen, among objects previously undervalued in historical explanation, and in that sense "new." It is to be found among lamps, coins, Arretine pottery, silver vessels, bronze furniture, private altars, terracotta revetments and other architectural details—all, uncovered by archeology, in aid of more traditional sources.

The third exception or illustration is A. R. Birley's life of Septimius Severus.[19] Within conventional narrative history it provides a model of the highest quality. Quite aside from the style, which is very much more than clear and agreeable, the subject himself is perfectly placed inside a family, a homeland, a circle of intimates aiding his rise; and, with these explained, the flow of events is intelligible, marking the long years of his leadership and his political and military struggles. What is to be noticed is the lucky coincidence between Birley's choice of subject, and the peak of production and survival of Latin inscriptions. Through these, not only a very rich amount of prosopography in the old style can be worked out, so as to give a surprisingly rich picture of the emperor's times, but in addition, all sorts of details can be woven into a context.

Then, too, there are other sources. Coarse-ware pot-sherds have a story to tell. In Severus' Tripolitanian homeland a Commission of Olive Oil-Procurement was established by him, connected with the expansion of the dole to the populace of the capital. As C. Panella showed for Q. Granius Caelestinus of Lepcis Magna in that region, and as other scholars showed for other leading figures of the city, they were in a position to supply the huge increase in need from their own orchards. One supplier was a Severan consul of 207; another, the praetorian prefect, Plautianus; but his stamped amphorae drop out of the

---

[19] *The African Emperor,* ed. 2 significantly revised (New Haven 1988).

archeological record just at the time of his eclipse in AD 205. The emperor's own harvests register in the same record, but with a corresponding upturn from that year. Meanwhile Lepcis benefited as never before from the rising tide of wealth, from which derived all sorts of improvements and amenities.[20] It is rare indeed to see so neatly entwined the lives of specific individuals, surviving buildings and streets, and the stories in Dio Cassius and elsewhere, all afloat on millions of litres of olive oil per annum.

The dynamic fortunes of Tripolitania, rich throughout the second century but dramatically more so toward the end and into the earlier third, register at Ostia in the Terme del Nuotatore. With extraordinary success, the coarse-ware sherds once used there as fill have now been analyzed to reveal the provenance, date, and contents of containers feeding a million Romans from Caesar's day up into that of the Antonines. Of course Tripolitanian amphorae appear in this context. The material as a whole, beginning to be used for broad historical interpretation in the 1970s by C. Panella and others, entered the Anglophone stream in the 1980s (and if Starr sometimes mentioned his own works in his survey, he may excuse my instancing myself at this point as one who profited from the Terme evidence).[21] The ability to quantify economic relationships, even where the results still need care in handling, enhanced the meaning of discussions both old and new, to a very great degree.

A. Tchernia's work on the wine trade combined the testimony of familiar writers, like Columella and the two Pliny's, with coarse-ware archeology, including the yield from Ostia.[22] As he was able to show, the huge export from Italy in the decades around the turn of the era had given way to import;

---

[20] See D. Manacorda, "Testimonianze sulla produzione e il consumo dell'olio tripolitano nel III secolo," *Dialoghi di archeologia* 9-10 (1976-77) 542f., using Panella, and used by Birley, (n.19) p. 18 (though perhaps not fully enough) and by D. J. Mattingly, *Tripolitania* (London 1995) 153ff. (with bibliog.).

[21] R. MacMullen, *Corruption and the Decline of Rome* (New Haven 1988) 11ff.

[22] *Le vin de l'Italie romaine: essai d'histoire économique d'après les amphores* (Rome 1986) making use of Ostian data (e.g. pp. 234ff., 247ff.); P. Arthur and D. Williams, "Campanian wine, Roman Britain and the third century," *JRA* 5 (1992) 250ff.; S. Martin-Kilcher, "Amphoren der späten Republik und der frühen Kaiserzeit in Karthago. Zu den Lebensmittelimporten der Colonia Iulia Concordia," *RM* 100 (1993) 269ff., esp. 291ff.

and from the mid-first century that line rose ever more sharply in Flavian times and after. A point needing to be considered in the resulting picture is that nullity, Domitian's edict to forbid Gallic viticulture. It serves to show the effectiveness, or rather the total lack of effect, of statute aimed at custom. Literary texts by themselves had been entirely misleading. Tchernia presents in fact a very complicated tableau, partly because of the separate histories of half a dozen major varieties of fine wines and productive regions. Clearly there is more qualification and nuancing to be expected as excavation continues; second- and third-century Italian amphorae reaching Britain, for example, call in question the supposed decline of Campanian production and export after the first century, on which large theories of social and economic change had been founded; or again, the reception of Italian wine in Africa and Spain and the competition from eastern vineyards need to be factored in. But the advances in the subject to date are nevertheless highly welcome.

And, for anyone wishing to understand better what the archeologists have to work with before they translate it into a tidier written form, there is just what the outsider needs: a beautifully clear and simple yet detailed introduction to the subject by two experts.[23]

How Rostovtzeff would have rejoiced had he had at his pen's tip all that is now available, and could have seen it so clearly once more in the news! For there is certainly a marked revival of the Social and Economic History of the Roman Empire in recent years. His prescience on display in the magnum opus of 1926 was remarkable; and it has often been remarked how much he anticipated the manner of writing history on which is founded the later fame of Braudel.

Recent discussion of his approach has focused on several related questions. They may be most conveniently outlined beginning with the more general, and so on to the more specific. The general may be traced to M. I. Finley's vision of the empire's total economy as primitive and close to the soil, little monetized, structurally different from the modern, compared to Rostovtzeff's vision of it as dynamic, elaborate, and, in its Mediterranean-wide markets and manufacture and the mind-set of the urban middle and upper classes, "up to date." Finley was

---

[23] D. P. S. Peacock and D. F. Williams, *Amphorae and the Roman Economy. An Introductory Guide* (London 1986).

by no means at his best in Roman empire studies, but his provocative way of presenting his ideas, and their intrinsic interest, aroused an active debate.[24]

At the level of method: Rostovtzeff's positivist approach and patience in assembling a thousand tesserae into a single mosaic was not for Finley. He ridiculed minutiae as the source of historical insights, reminding his readers of Wheeler's anecdote about the 39 sherds: a basis for some scholary inference, but they all turned out to belong to a single pot. "The still prevalent antiquarian procedure of listing all known discrete 'facts' is no method at all." What was indeed needed was quantification; but it couldn't be found in the archeological record, as he saw it. Better, then, to generate the equivalent of quantification through models, orders of magnitude, and comparison with other socio-economic worlds in broad terms.

The most basic question was of course how big or powerful the total economy was. It was important to establish this since, by an obvious train of reasoning, the empire owed its initial size and historical impact to conquest and the defense of what it had gained; the armed forces were the instrument thereof; their cost limited their size and thus their historical impact; so that the capacity to generate wealth and direct it through taxes to this instrument was of the essence. In the 1980s, after a faulty attempt at an estimate of the economy over-all, a second was made more successfully—the work of R. W. Goldsmith. A comparative economist, his previous publication had lain in quite distant areas and periods.[25] Non-specialists might well

---

[24] *The Ancient Economy*, ed. 2 (London 1985) including chap. 7, "Further thoughts" in rebuttal of objections raised to the first edition. Quoted on "facts," 194, in his discussion of the correct "model of the city;" idem, "The ancient city: from Fustel de Coulanges to Max Weber and beyond," *Comparative Studies in Society and History* 19 (1977) 324, "positivistic" as a term of criticism, almost of dismissal, and (325) dismissive of the value of studies of individual cities.

[25] "An estimate of the size and structure of the national product of the early Roman empire," *Review of Income and Wealth* 30 (1984) 263ff., quoted at 269; wealth distribution, comparing the U.S., p. 286; and at p. 273 gently reproaches a previous GNP underestimate (by 2 1/2 times!). He has gone on to expand on his findings, in chap. 4 of his *Premodern Financial Systems. A Historical Comparative Study* (Cambridge 1987) at p. 56 estimating the contribution of the land to the Roman GNP. His work is used in MacMullen (n.21), B. W. Frier's review, *JRA* 4 (1991) 245, D.P. Kehoe, *Management and Investment on Estates in Roman Egypt during the Early Empire* (Bonn 1992) 1, W. V. Harris, "Between archaic and modern: some current problems in the history of the Roman economy," in idem (ed), *The Inscribed*

misunderstand his saying that "an estimate with a margin of error of 50 percent is better than no figure at all;" and then, too, his results were first offered in a journal ancient historians never look at; yet despite their coming into play from left-field, so to speak, they have begun to exert their influence on a variety of topics. It is not only the meaning of army size that depends on his findings (or others' findings, as they may be improved in the future). They must be considered also, for example, in any discussion of the empire's internal stability. There are obvious sociopolitical implications in wealth distribution (and perhaps little comfort to ourselves in the fact that the disparity in income between the average Roman and one of those incredible senators was far less than between the average American today and the corresponding percentage of the super-rich in our own society).

Goldsmith posits that some 60% of the empire's GNP was generated by agriculture. That too is a figure with obvious implications. In particular, it bears on Finley's minimalist views and on the character of Roman cities as he pictured them. Did they earn much money for themselves, perhaps a third or more, through trade and manufacture? Or were they only consumers of what rentier citizens contributed through gifts and spending? The two different visions have a history in fact reaching back well before Rostovtzeff.[26] While Finley saw no prospect of enlightenment in the study of individual cities, W. Jongman and D. Engels have gone ahead anyway, respectively examining

---

*Economy. Production and Distribution in the Roman Empire in the Light of Instrumentum Domesticum* (Ann Arbor 1993) 20 n.68 (dismissing one point of Goldsmith's discussion or again, in F. Millar's wonderful survey of *The Roman Near East 31 BC-AD 337* (Cambridge 1993) 49, or K. W. Harl, *Coinage in the Roman Economy, 300 B.C. to A.D. 700* (Baltimore 1996) 410.

[26] See esp. H. Bruhns, "De Werner Sombart à Max Weber et Moses I. Finley," *L'origine des richesses dépensées dans la ville antique* (Aix 1985) 255ff., raising the question, what group or interest made decisions for the city, quite apart from its real sources of livelihood. Further discussion in W. Jongman, *The Economy and Society of Pompeii* (Amsterdam 1988), in his first hundred pages or so, and 192-99, arguing for a consumer-city model at least in Italy; also D. Engels, *Roman Corinth. An Alternative Model for the Classical City* (Chicago 1990) esp. in his opening pages; good quick review of French contributions in G. Tate, *Les campagnes de la Syrie du Nord du IIe au VIIe siecle. Un exemple d' expansion démographique et économique à la fin d'Antiquité, 1* (Paris 1992) 9f.; a mass of hard data in small bits in R. Duncan-Jones, *Money and Government in the Roman Empire* (Cambridge 1994); and a really excellent overview by W. V. Harris (n.25).

Pompeii and Corinth in great detail and with much sophistication of method.

On the looser question of the sources of wealth and the contribution of trade and manufacture, Finley's claim that we have no useful numbers to serve our analysis ignored the graffiti of La Graufesenque. They had been long familiar through handbooks on the ancient economy.[27] Part of their interest lay, of course, in their showing that the work force included slaves only in menial positions, almost invisibly, and not numerous. The potters themselves, 131 out of some hundreds known by their names on their product, earned a modest living, most of them, except those few who owned kilns and fired the pots of the others. They formed themselves into associations with a presiding deity and priest, as working men so commonly did in the Roman world. Monthly firings took care of ten to forty thousand vessels; the totals were noted on wasters used as scratchpaper; and here, another part of the interest of La Graufesenque. A cluster of structures crudely put together in an unnoticed corner of Gaul, at the service of a loosely organized tiny village (as it must have appeared), produced a million articles a year and more, of high value, for export all around Gaul, Britain, Spain, Germany, north Africa, Italy including Pompeii at the moment of its burial; also, Egypt, Syria, Greece, Palestine, the shores of the Black Sea; and this, all, over the span of a century. The modern expectation that great production must mean a factory, a regiment of toilers at the wheels, capitalist owners, and so forth, isn't answered in the slightest; no more would it be in the iron-producing villages of Noricum at the time or, so far as regards physical facilities, in the very emperor's mints.

On the Spanish markets the terra sigillata of Gaul was displaced by a native equivalent, of which the principal points

---

[27] E.g. A. Grenier in T. Frank, (ed), *An Economic Survey of Ancient Rome* 3 (Baltimore 1937) 543ff.; now, A. Vernhet, "Présentation générale," in J.-P. Jacob and C. Bemont, (edd), *La terre sigillé gallo-romaine: lieux de production du Haut Empire: implantations, produits, relations* (Paris 1986) 32ff.; idem, ibid. 39ff., "L'essor des ateliers entre 30 et 120 ap. J.-C."; R. Marichal, "Nouveaux aperçus sur la vie et la structure des ateliers de la Graufesenque d'après les comptes de potiers," ibid. 17ff.; idem, *Les graffites de la Graufesenque* (Paris 1988) esp. 106ff. For another later production center as yet unexcavated, see M. Mackensen, "Prospektion einer spätantiken Sigillatatöpferei in El Mahrin, Nordtunesien," CEDAC *Carthage Bulletin* 6 (1985) 29f., of ca. 360-480, likewise of wide markets despite the unimpressive site.

of production are now identified. By far the largest was centered in a cluster of kilns strung along a few miles of the Ebro valley at Tritium Magallum.[28] The artisan population and facilities very closely resemble those of La Graufesenque (and a number of other much smaller Gallic and Spanish production points as well)—perhaps on a slightly larger scale, and able, from the Flavians on, to displace Gallic terra sigillata not only in the peninsula but in Mauretania as well. Despite this productive power, the hundreds of potters, here too, were a humble folk. Only a half dozen stood out in wealth, even then, insufficient to appear in the epigraphy of the province. Yet public office was held in other towns by natives of Tritium Magallum: grown rich as middlemen? The question, very far from clear at the moment, has nevertheless a clear bearing on that other, above: whether or in what way the city was a mere consumer of wealth produced on the land.

And a footnote to the matter of productivity: misunderstandings about the remarkable Barbegal watermill, on which various theories had been based, were recently corrected; further, an African waterwheel of a sophisticated design was identified; and a broad study concluded that "the waterwheel was one of the ordinary features of a village, fort, or large villa wherever [in northern Gaul] the hydrographic situation allowed."[29] Notice "ordinary".

W. V. Harris in his most valuable review of the empire's economy pulls out for mention a second-century "single import shipment" appearing in a papyrus text published in the 1980s, including six million sesterces' worth of nard and ivory, "more than the retail value of the grain carried by twenty large merchant ships."[30] The instance of the scale is very suggestive;

---

[28] F. Mayet, *Les céramiques sigillées hispaniques: Contributions à l'histoire économique de la péninsule Ibérique sous l'Empire Romain*, 2 vols. (Paris 1984) esp. 59ff., 216ff., with a town official in Merida and a flamen in Italica, *ILS* 1626 and ILER 6398.

[29] P. Leveau, "The Barbegal water mill in its environment: archeology and the economic and social history of antiquity," *JRA* 9 (1996) 137ff., this first industrial use of water power dating to ca. Trajan; A. T. Hodge, "A Roman factory," *Scientific American* Nov. 1990, 106ff., with excellent drawings; A. Wilson, "Water-power in North Africa and the development of the horizontal water-wheel," *JRA* 8 (1995) 499ff., a sophisticated device in the Medjerda valley, ca. 300; and G. Rapsaet, "Les prémices de la mécanisation agricole entre Seine et Rhin de l'Antiquité au 13e siècle," *Annales* 50 (1995) 911, 916 quoted.

[30] N.25, 12.

yet statements based on this and similar if less striking data are too few to produce more than adjectival, not numerical, characterizations. So long as that is the case, point after point of discussion of the economy, Harris' or Goldsmith's or any other, will seem wrong or at least questionable to competent scholars. So Clio must rock in her chair for a time yet.

As a specific illustration: the question, to what extent was the economy monetized?—meaning, among other things, how much coinage was available to be used. Harris dismisses Goldsmith's guesses as nothing more than that; R. Duncan-Jones' very ingenious chapter on the conclusions to be drawn from coin hoards is subjected to damaging attack by C. Howgego;[31] and venturing now among the Clashing Rocks, the much-to-be-feared scholarly Symplegades, comes K. W. Harl with relevant pages in his hugely comprehensive and welcome book on Roman coins.[32] His is generally a maximalist or Rostovtzeffian view of the economy as a whole, influenced as he is by his estimates of die-capacity and numbers of issues. For example, "Diocletian alone directed a recoinage on a scale that dwarfed all coinages until this century." Long before that point, Augustus had established a (western) world currency, inundating the markets from Britain, where Cunobelinus struck gold coins on the Roman scale, to Asia Minor, where city mints likewise adopted Roman equivalencies.

Returning my review of the empire's economy to its starting point in rural productivity, Tripolitanian or other, there are the studies of African great estates by P. Ørsted and D. P. Kehoe, following on the latter's similar study of Egyptian farms[33]; and, regarding both north Africa and Italy, J. P. Vallat has examined "The place and role of the *Annales* school in an approach to the Roman rural economy," emphasizing how recent has been the

---

[31] Above, n.25; C. Howgego's review, *JRS* 86 (1996) 208f., of Duncan-Jones, (n.20), chaps. 5-6.

[32] *Coinage in the Roman Economy, 300 B.C. to A.D. 700* (Baltimore 1996) 3 on Diocletian; chap. 3 on the Augustan currency; and M. G. Fulford, "Demonstrating Britannia's economic dependence in the first and second centuries," *Military and Civilian in Roman Britain*, T. F. C. Blagg and A. C. King, (edd), (Oxford 1984) 130f. on Cymbeline's aureus.

[33] Ørsted, "From Henchir Mettich to the Albertini Tablets. A study in the economic and social significance of the Roman lease system (locatio-conductio)," *Landuse in the Roman Empire*, J. Carlsen *et al.*, (edd), (Rome 1994) 115ff.; Kehoe, cit. above (n.25) and *The Economics of Agriculture on Roman Imperial Estates in North Africa* (Gottingen 1988) asking (3) if the word "rational" applies.

inclusion of the ancient world in the school's work, and how it has tied in to discussion of technological supremacy, alleged. In fact, the elaborate exploitation of arid land shows "it was Rome that admired the 'African hydraulicians' and not the other way round; it was not Rome that brought either terracing or irrigation methods."[34]

Ideas about how best to profit from the means within one's control depend, of course, on definitions of "profit." Those will vary according to the society. They need not lie within the bounds of purely economic value, maximum money in familiar capitalist terms. Kehoe wonders if the Roman habits of mind in this respect would count in our terms as "rational," since simple security of investment was so large a consideration (and it has long been acknowledged that the respectability of some forms of wealth over others influenced the Roman elite's economic behavior to a marked degree). Even more striking was the manner in which the rich spent their surplus, through evergetism. This, the great engine of their civilization, has received much attention in recent decades, but in no more stimulating treatment than P. Veyne's, now Englished.[35] He brings to bear an extraordinarily active mind, sympathetic imagination, and wide reading which carries the reader unexpectedly to analogies in Brazilian elections, or wherever or whatever. A specimen of his style, concerning relations between the supreme evergete, the emperor, and his public, may suggest the qualities of the book:

> The Column [of Trajan] is no more propaganda than the Gothic cathedrals were visual catechisms. It is ornamented with reliefs showing figures because, being a monument, it could not exist without speaking or speak without saying something. It therefore contains a message; it tells in detail of Trajan's campaigns so as to express his glory, but this detail seems to have interested the sculptor himself more than it interests the passers-by. It is with Imperial majesty as with the star-strewn sky that expresses the glory of God. What is more expressive than the sky? But in order to perceive its expression we do not need to itemize the stars one by one.... The ruling power obtained additional prestige from the very irrationality of its expressions, which spoke for themselves, and were proudly indifferent to their audience. Grandiloquent nonsense has always been the privilege and sign of gods, oracles, and 'bosses.'

---

[34] In *The Annales School and Archeology*, J. Bintliff, (ed), (Leicester 1991) 73ff.; quoted, 79f.

[35] *Bread and Circuses. Historical Sociology and Political Pluralism*, trans. B. Pearce (London 1990) from the 1976 ed., *Le pain et le cirque* (with some excisions, reminding me of my own vain earlier efforts to arrange an unabbreviated translation).

'Affective' historiography focusing on the reasons for human action—on the behavior of great men toward the masses of their fellow citizens, for example, and therefore on the 'mentalité' that supports a given form of government, imperial or municipal—appears increasingly in the literature, witness the work of Zanker, above. It takes a certain courage, such as Veyne here demonstrates, to assert what the truth must be, out of one's knowledge of human behavior, even where demonstration is impossible; for there happens to be no explicit statement, no results of questionaires and polls. Instead, the material on which an interpretation must be built is made up of testimonia that mean what they mean because one cannot imagine otherwise; and emphasis is on the verb *imagine*. But what sort of proof is that!?

Such a method has of course not supplanted more traditional approaches. Of these, F. Quass offers an excellent specimen: concerned with political climate and expressions at the municipal level and in the eastern provinces, much concerned therefore with evergetism among other matters, amazed, rightly, at its force, but tying his discussion far more closely to his evidence. Here is one of those reassuring studies in which the footnotes' bulk considerably exceeds that of the text. [36]

One may stay very close to hard evidence, stony-hard, as Zanker did, and still reveal the most delicate truths. W. L. MacDonald, best of architectural historians who has long known how to make the ancient bricks and marble sing, has applied the same magic, with the collaboration of J. L. Pinto, to Hadrian's villa.[37] Considering what anyone might have supposed about the fame and familiarity of the site, the results advance our understanding to an astonishing degree. Not only is the whole history of the villa narrated, down to the present with its echoes in Le Corbusier or Frank Lloyd Wright, and comparisons usefully drawn to other, lesser Roman structures of

---

[36] *Die Honoratiorenschicht in den Städten des griechischen Ostens. Untersuchungen zur politischen und sozialen Entwicklung in hellenistischer und römischer Zeit* (Stuttgart 1993) 49ff., 373ff., and passim; 300, "die erstaunliche Leistungsbereitschaft der Honoratioren...." A second good example with a similar approach, closely text-based yet aimed at explaining perceptions and mentalities, is M.W. Gleason's *Making Men. Sophists and Self-Presentation in Ancient Rome* (Princeton 1995).

[37] Cit. above (n.17), e.g. 114ff. (esthetic effects), 170ff. (waterworks), chap. 7 on occupants, and p. 330, quoted.

the same sort; not only is the largely forgotten entirety of the site given fair treatment, and all sorts of details made interesting; but beyond this level of the meticulous, the esthetics receive full, almost empathetic, explanation. The villa as in fact a village is explained, as well, with its own defense force (perhaps two praetorian cohorts) and seven or eight hundred servants. Also, the wonderful waterworks. And so on. "What monument says more about that [Roman] world than the villa?"

At the absolutely opposite extreme, not sumptuous and central but impoverished and peripheral, the empire's desert rims to the south and east have recently become known and better understood, thanks to archeology—some of it conventional, some from the air.[38] The choice of the southern area for study is very much of the *Annales* school, involved in questions of political and cultural imperialism, the least familiar patterns of subsistence, and comparative anthropology. As to the eastern rim, however, the attraction may lie in its being relatively little explored, with corresponding rewards for excavation by S. T. Parker and others; also, in the challenge offered by E. N. Luttwak.[39]

Luttwak's picture of the empire's frontier history was promptly acknowledged to be novel and stimulating though unrecognizable as Roman, in various important respects (he approached it not as a Roman historian but as a defense analyst); or, contrariwise, the book was praised as just what Roman studies needed.[40] Certainly it generated a great deal of

---

[38] Giving access to recent advances in knowledge of the east, notice S. T. Parker, *Romans and Saracens: A History of the Arabian Frontier* (Winona Lake 1986); D. Kennedy and D. Riley, *Rome's Desert Frontier from the Air* (London 1990); and M. MacDonald, "Nomads and the Hawrân in the Late Hellenistic and Roman periods," *Syria* 70 (1993) 303-403 (which I have not seen); on the south, with engagement in the question of modes of subsistence, R. B. Hitchner, "The changing face of pastoralism in the Tunisian high steppe," *Landuse in the Roman Empire,* J. Carlsen *et al.,* (edd), (Rome 1994) 27ff.; N. Ferchiou, "Nouvelles données sur un fossé inconnu en Afrique proconsulaire et sur la *Fossa Regia,*" *Histoire et archéologie de l'Afrique du Nord: Actes du III^e Colloque international, Montpellier...1985* (Paris 1986) 351ff.; and various substantial studies by B. D. Shaw collected in his *Environment and Society in Roman North Africa: Studies in History and Archaeology* and *Rulers, Nomads, and Christians in Roman North Africa* (both of Aldershot 1995).

[39] *The Grand Strategy of the Roman Empire: From the First Century to the Third* (Baltimore 1976).

[40] *AHR* 82 (1977) 930f., pretty unfavorable; favorable, P. A. Brunt. F. Millar, and many others, cf. C. R. Whittaker, *Frontiers of the Roman Empire. A Social and*

discussion in the 1980s and 1990s, in which Whittaker's and
Isaac's books, with Wheeler's very long essay, stand out. In
view of the latter, however, and with mention of other very
helpful shorter reviews by good authorities,[41] perhaps no more
than a resume is needed here.

In brief, the image of Hadrian's Wall and similar
fortifications between Rhine and Danube and in north Africa
once invited a certain way of picturing "the frontier"—a line
dividing what anyone would call "Rome" or "the empire" from
outsiders. Further digging, however, has revealed structures
variously disposed and variously shaped along this line, or more
often no line at all, constituting more truly a zone. It was
Luttwak's aim to arrange both line and zone in an explanatory
framework across time; but his explanation was open to many
criticisms, in particular those drawing on "the fantastic
explosion of data that archeological research has generated"
since the publication of his book. In time, criticisms provoked
his defenders. The back and forth of "the scholarly pendulum,"
in Wheeler's phrase, or Clio's chair, was set in motion. It is not
at present clear just where consensus may emerge and where at
other points our data will finally prove inadequate for that end.

What is most important and most problematical are
questions of intent: for example, did the Romans (and exactly
which ones were in a position to make decisions, and how?)
wish to move forward (in all periods? on all fronts?), or were
their military forces rather meant to insure non-military
objectives? According to what perceptions of the outsiders or
provincial populations were Roman decisions made? Toward
what ends or benefits? Chester Starr already noted a special
concentration of interest in frontier studies, but they have since
led on to questions about imperialism in all its aspects. Many
loose ends are obvious at the present date still.

At the heart of the empire I choose for mention a final topic,
religion. Publication here continues at a great rate, especially
manifest in the long series of EPRO: "Preliminary Studies on

---

*Economic Study* (Baltimore 1994) 286; B. Isaac, *The Limits of Empire: The Roman
Army in the East* (Oxford 1990); and E. L. Wheeler, "Methodological limits and the
mirage of Roman strategy," *Jnl of Military Hist.* 57 (1993) 7ff., 215, 216
("pendulum"), and passim. To the eastern flank of the subject, Millar (cit., above
n.25) supplies important background, e.g. at 141 and 183f.

[41] S. T. Parker, *JRA* 5 (1992); C. M. Wells, ibid. 9 (1996) 436ff., and P. Freeman,
*Britannia* 27 ( 1996) 465ff., esp. 463, "explosion of data".

Oriental Religions." Notice the by-now-extraordinary first word: well over a hundred volumes of mere warm-ups! The whole project responds to the inspiration offered by Cumont toward the end of the nineteenth century, deeply influencing so many scholars after him. His influence has lost force; but there linger those of the old teaching like R. Turcan who still begin with "Cumont…this book pays tribute to the master," and who continue along the lines long since characterized, rightly, as reflecting only a Christian definition of religion: "a religion is unsuccessful only if it can monopolize the individual totally: body and soul"—as opposed to the "finicky ritualism" of Roman cults.[42] Interpretation aside (!) Turcan's work is meticulous and informative, though only on the eastern provinces' cults. Of these in turn, of course the one that Cumont made news with, Mithraism, continues to generate conferences and articles. The Cumontane derivation of this, directly and in one flow from Iran, is now slowly giving way to the view that the flow was interrupted and Mithraism of the empire was in fact a re-invention, possibly at Rome, possibly in a Danube province, with its own distinct character; so that it can't be understood by going back to supposed roots in an eastern homeland.[43]

Other advances in interpretation have been secured by S. R. F. Price's excellent work on the imperial cult. Speaking of religious rituals which we know best in the eastern provinces (though his dictum applies throughout the empire), on the subject of cult banquets he says, "It is a mistake to think that all banquets at this period were secular in tone… [It is] a false problem. Modern scholars wrongly tend to divide what was a single Greek semantic field into two and to distinguish between religious and secular aspects. The Greeks did not do this."[44] He goes on to rescue the imperial cult from the hands of those modern scholars who cannot believe it (yet the masses "took the

---

[42] R. Turcan, *The Cults of the Roman Empire*, trans. A. Nevill (Oxford 1996) (with its misleading translation of the French title, *Les cultes orientaux dans le monde Romain* (Paris 1992). I quote from 7 and 22 to show the echoes of Nock and of those persuaded by Nock's 1933 *Conversion*.

[43] See e.g. A. Blomart, "Mithra: quoi de neuf en 1990," *JRA* 9 (1996) 427f.

[44] "Between man and god: sacrifice in the Roman empire," *JRS* 70 (1980) 41, repeated in his *Rituals and Power: Imperial Cult in Asia Minor* (Cambridge 1985) 230; on his use of terms of affect in worship, notice 104, 190, 213, 233, 244, quoted; and 115f. on seriousness.

cult seriously," with "complete seriousness," not "skepticism").
The problem, here as with rituals, is our Christian mind-set. He
goes on to correct the Christianizing of interpretation at other
points, including the tendency always to look for, and not find,
religious experiences which are best known to us from the road
to Damascus. The sentence quoted from Turcan, above, may
stand for the older style. But, in correcting it and denying any
affective aspect of belief in paganism, one may go too far and
so throw out the baby with the bath. Price rightly retains terms
like "rapture", "adoration", "dependence", "gratitude", "joy",
and "genuine piety" in his vocabulary of interpretation.

P. Brown has kept a popular focus on religion especially in
the later empire, with his marvelously elegant evocations of
religiosity. He writes about asceticism especially. It has,
however, been pointed out by W. Treadgold that what Brown
offers at the center of his picture, holy men and "the holy," are
in fact phenomena of very little currency or familiarity to the
world in which they are found, however great their interest may
then have been to certain audiences or may be to us today.[45]

On the other hand, Treadgold himself leaves out of *his*
picture a major phenomenon, post-Constantinian paganism in
the eastern empire, to which F. R. Trombley has drawn very
welcome attention—welcome, since the actual dimensions of
the subject had been almost entirely ignored by everyone
earlier.[46] The story in the western regions has been equally
disregarded. In fact, so argues my own study, the whole of
paganism was partly persecuted and suppressed by the church,
partly folded around Christianity, in a story of much
significance and vitality running up through the reign of
Charlemagne and his contemporary emperors in
Constantinople.[47]

Two further contributions to late Roman studies are to be
credited respectively to a single author, and to a group:
meaning, at last, an intelligible account of the Goths where
before there had been only confusion and obscurity—this first

---

[45] W. Treadgold, "Taking sources on their own terms and on ours; Peter Brown's
Late Antiquity," *Antiquité tardive* 2 (1994) 156.

[46] Ibid. 155, "Christians...by the sixth century were just about everyone," since
"the Christianization of the empire was nearly complete" by mid-fifth; cf.Trombley's
*Hellenic Religion and Christianization c. 370-529*, 2 vols. (Leiden 1993-94).

[47] *Christianity and Paganism in the Fourth to Eighth Centuries* (New Haven
1997).

advance thanks to H. Wolfram[48]—and, second, a revised view
of the "Decline" especially in the eastern half of the empire, as
it has emerged from a great deal of recent archeology. It is now
well established that the fortunes of Roman north Africa
attained a new height in the second half of the fourth century;[49]
and a variety of archeological approaches have revealed most
areas of the eastern empire likewise to have flourished in the
same period and later, that is, to the later fifth or early sixth
century depending on region.[50] What is striking is the
unexpected demographic curve upward, whereas, in the west,
the assertion of a contrary curve by A. E. R. Boak long ago
seems nowadays more reasonable.[51] Finley directed one of his
most destructive attacks at Boak, whose questions and answers,
both, were thereafter forgotten—most unfortunately for our
field of study.

To maintain some balance of attention, I revert from
increments of data on the archeological side, to those on the
philological side: to the recovery, beyond the Bar Kokhba Cave
documents and the Vindolanda tablets (above, n. 7), of works of
Diogenes of Oinoanda and Sidonius' verse epitaph, both on
stone, and of a substantial number of Augustine's most
interesting letters.[52] The list of discoveries of texts could be
extended by quite a number of items of considerable
significance to the history of the empire.

---

[48] *Geschichte der Goten: von den Anfängen bis zur Mittel des sechsten
Jahrhunderts. Entwurf einer historischen Ethnographie* (Munich 1979 = *History of
the Goths,* revised ed., trans. T. J. Dunlap, Berkeley 1988).

[49] The fullest revision in C. Lepelley, *Les cités de l'Afrique romaine au Bas-
Empire,* 2 vols. (Paris 1979-81); much recent support, e.g. in C. Witschel, "Die
Entwicklung der Gesellschaft von Timgad im 2. bis 4. Jh. n. Chr.," *Klio* 77 (1995)
275, or D. J. Mattingly and R. B. Hitchner, "Roman Africa: an archaeological
review," *JRS* 85 (1995) 210ff.

[50] MacMullen, *Corruption* cit. (n. 21) 31ff.; more recent support, e. g., Tate (n.26),
170-188, 303-32.

[51] L. Wierschowski, "Die historische Demographie—ein Schlüssel zur
Geschichte? Bevölkerungsrückgang und Krise des römischen Reiches im 3. Jh. n.
Chr.," *Klio* 76 (1994) 356, 376, and passim.

[52] M. F. Smith, "Diogenes of Oinoanda, new fragments 122-124," *Anatolian
Studies* 34 (1984) 43ff., A. Casanova, *I frammenti di Diogene d'Enoanda* (Florence
1984) and P. Gordon, *Epicurus in Lycia: The Second-Century World of Diogenes of
Oenoanda* (Ann Arbor 1996); F. Prévot, "Deux fragments de l'épitaphe de Sidoine
Apollinaire découverts à Clermont-Ferrand," *Antiquité tardive* 1 (1993) 223ff.; and
H. Chadwick, "New sermons of St Augustine," *JTS* 47 (1996) 69ff.

\* \* \*

At the end, I emphasize again that change in the focus of interest in the empire of which Chester Starr took note: the diminishing importance of political narrative, *histoire évènementielle,* and therefore of prosopography that served it, matched by a rising interest in cultural, social, and economic history.

In service to these latter areas, the *Annales* can be thanked for a great deal that is at least of heuristic value. Ancient historians can find in its pages much to make them think, "Why don't *we* try this?" On the other hand, Annalism has its absurdities and misapplications like any other approach. No need to pick out particular illustrations—but I quote again the reminder about basics offered by Duby and Perrot (at n. 14): history does and should concern itself with things that "influence events and social change." Add, that ours is a discipline. So it is undisciplined and in that sense bad history to take up a reader's time on subjects like lefthandedness, no matter how little noticed they may have been in the past or how exquisitely sophisticated one's discussion of them may be, with graphs and tables and calculations of statistical deviation.

Quantification is undeniably essential where useful information comes only in tiny bits, each of only tiny import; and exactly that will be the case with topics in society, culture, and economy. Both the written information base and the artifactual must be searched. Percentages of *tria nomina,* particular adjectives in epitaphs, or types of cases at law must be catalogued, numbers of potsherds, wasters, sunken vessels, or oil-presses must be added together in support of any conclusion worth stating.

Very good. But still, the results are likely to be descriptive rather than explanatory. Historians want also to understand motive: not just what patterns of investment or expenditure or wealth distribution can be documented, what pattern of frontier defense works, but the impulses they express. Only written evidence can offer any direct help, here, whether epigraphic or expecially literary; and the material will be still made up of "tiny bits." Care must be taken to distinguish between anecdotes that were interesting to contemporaries, *ben trovato,* and thus embroidered or invented, as opposed to those little glimpses or incidents that interest only ourselves and are therefore unlikely to have been worked up.[53]

Then, inevitably, we add guesswork. In consequence, compared to descriptive, quantifiable history, affective history can only appear very unscientific and in that sense unsophisticated. If it works, it is only through the historian imagining how people must have felt, and in turn finding an echo to his intuition among his readers. For illustration, Zanker's or Veyne's books, or my own *Corruption...*, attempting in its core chapter to describe and explain what power was and how it worked within the empire. Veyne draws the distinction between "the art of clearing up problems as opposed to the gift of sniffing out the presence of unsuspected ones;" and "sniffing out" suggests some of the delicacy or, if you will, the subjective, intuitive nature of much of his best work.[54]

It is likely that advances on this plane of thinking will continue to claim a rising share of our interest in Roman empire research.

---

[53] R. P. Saller, "Anecdotes as historical evidence for the Principate," *G&R* 27 (1980) 69ff., dealing with only the *ben trovato*.

[54] *Le quotidien et l'intesserant* (Paris 1995) 45. Further, P. Garnsey, "The generosity of Veyne," *JRS* 81 (1991) 164ff., esp. 167f. on Veyne's denial that history is a science or has a distinctive method; rather, that it is a diversion, it should be "fun".

# V

## GENERAL BIBLIOGRAPHY

In a work whose main purpose is to provide current and useful references, an additional list may seem superfluous. However, many of the references in the individual chapters point to specific subjects and, since this volume is intended for a variety of readers, the following titles are more general publications that have wider applicability.

*L'Année philologique (1928 - ).*
> The annual bibliography of publications in all aspects of classical studies dating from 1928.

*Aufstieg und Niedergang der römischen Welt* (Berlin 1972 - ).
> Articles are in several languages, including English. The subtitle defines the purpose: to present the history and culture of Rome in light of new research.

Boardman, John et al. (eds.), *The Oxford History of the Classical World* (Oxford, 1988)

*Cambridge Ancient History*, 2d ed. (Cambridge, 1982 -).

*Der Kleine Pauly* (Stuttgart 1964-75): an abbreviated and updated form of the massive *Real-Encyclopädie der classischen Altertumswissenschaft*, edited by Pauly and Wissowa.

*Der Neue Pauly* (Stuttgart 1996; so far volume I has been published).

*Guide to Historical Literature* of the American Historical Association,. 3d ed, vol. 1 (New York 1995)

Hornblower, Simon and Anthony Spawford, *Oxford Classical Dictionary*, 3d ed. (Oxford and New York, 1996)

Matthew, B., ed., *Dictionary of the Roman Empire* (Oxford, 1995)

*The Oxford Dictionary of Byzantium*, 3d ed., 3 vols. (New York and Oxford, 1991)

*Penguin Historical Atlases*, recently revised:

    *Ancient Rome* by C. Scarre (Harmondsworth, 1995)

    *Ancient Greece* by R. Morkot (Harmondsworth, 1996)

Pollitt, J. J., *The Art of Rome c. 753 B.C.-A.D. 337: Sources and Documents* (Cambridge, 1983)

Settis, S. (ed.), *I Greci: Storia, cultura, arte, società* (Turin 1995ff.; so far I and II.1). I: *Greece and the Hellenistic World* (Oxford 1988).

# CONTRIBUTORS

**Stanley M. Burstein** is currently Professor of History and Chair of the Department of History at California State University, Los Angeles. He was educated at the University of California, Los Angeles, receiving his Ph.D. in 1972. Winner of several fellowships and grants from the National Endowment for the Humanities, he holds the record for service to the AAH: two terms as secretary-treasurer and one term as president for a total of nine years.

His area of research is Hellenistic history with particular emphasis on issues involving Greek relations with Egypt and its neighbors. Among his publications are: *Outpost of Hellenism: The Emergence of Heraclea on the Black Sea* (Berkeley and Los Angeles, 1976); *The Babyloniaca of Berossus* (Malibu 1978); *The Hellenistic Age from the Battle of Ipsos to the Death of Kleopatra VII* (Cambridge 1985); *Agatharchides of Cnidus. On the Erythraean Sea* (London 1989); *Graeco-Africana: Studies in the History of Greek Relations with Egypt and Nubia* (New Rochelle 1995) and (with D. B. Nagle) *The Ancient World: Readings in Social and Cultural History* (Upper Saddle River 1995). He is currently part of a team writing a new history of Greece to be published by Oxford University Press.

**Ramsay MacMullen** took his B.A., M.A. and Ph.D. (1957) at Harvard University, taught European history at the University of Oregon and Brandeis, with specialization in the classical period, and moved to Yale in 1967. There he taught Roman history, as Dunham Professor of History and Classics from 1979 until his retirement in 1993. Among his more recent books are *Paganism in the Roman Empire* (New Haven 1981); *Corruption and the Decline of Rome* (New Haven 1988); *Christianity and Paganism in the Fourth to Eighth Centuries* (New Haven 1997);

and selected shorter studies under the title *Changes in the Roman Empire: Essays in the Ordinary* (Princeton 1990).

He has been a member of the AAH since its inception, its members elected him to serve as its second president, and he has been a constant champion of the Association's responsibility to establish and retain contacts with as large as possible segment of students and teachers of ancient history, a bargaining chip in gaining his essay for this volume!

**Kurt A. Raaflaub** on receiving his PhD at the University of Basel, Switzerland (1970), taught at the Freie Universität Berlin from 1972-78 then moved to Brown University in 1978 where he is currently Professor of Classics and History. With Deborah Boedeker, he is also joint director of the Center for Hellenic Studies in Washington, D.C.

His main interests—the social, political and intellectual history of archaic and classical Greece and the social and political history of the early and late Roman Republic and early empire—are reflected in his publications which include: *Dignitatis contentio: Motivation and Political Strategy in Caesar's Civil War* (Munich 1974 in German); and *The Discovery of Freedom* (Munich 1985 in German; 2d ed in English in preparation); he has edited and coauthored *Social Struggles in Archaic Rome* (Berkeley 1986); *Between Republic and Empire: Interpretations of Augustus and his Principate* (Berkeley 1990); *City-States in Classical Antiquity and Medieval Italy* (Stuttgart and Ann Arbor 1991); *Beginnings of Political Thought in the Ancient World: The Near-Eastern Civilizations and the Greeks* (Munich 1993, in German). His current projects include *Odysseus in a New World: Homer and Early Greek Society* and *Early Greek Political Thought.*

He has organized several international colloquia and conferences, including the annual meeting of the AAH in 1989.

**Allen Ward** received his B.A. from Brown and did his graduate work at Princeton where he was awarded the Ph.D. in 1968. He taught for two years at Columbia and since 1969 has been at the University of Connecticut with appointments in history and classics. His focus is Roman history, the late Republic in particular.

Among his publications are "The Early Relationships between Cicero and Pompey to 80 B.C.", *Phoenix* 24 (1970) 119-29; *Marcus Crassus and the Late Roman Republic*

(Columbia 1977); *A History of the Roman People* (2d ed., Englewood Cliffs, 1984) with Heichelheim and Yeo; *A Brief History of Rome and its Multi-cultural Civilization to A.D. 565* (Amherst 1995). Currently he is preparing the third edition of *A History of the Roman People*.

Allen's efforts in expanding interest in antiquity is evidenced by his direction of the Summer Institute in Classical Humanities for the Classical Association of New England eight times from 1985 through 1993. He was awarded the Barlow-Beach distinguished service award from that Association. For the AAH he has recently taken on the sometimes-difficult task of preserving parliamentary order at the annual business meetings.

# THE ASSOCIATION OF ANCIENT HISTORIANS

The Association of Ancient Historians had its origins in 1969 when faculty members from the State University of New York at Buffalo, McMaster University, and the University of Toronto met at McMaster to present papers and discuss topics of mutual interest. Over the next five years, annual meetings were organized at SUNY-Buffalo, the University of Michigan, Penn State University, the University of North Carolina, Duke University, and Ohio State University. During this period the annual meetings were enlarged and transformed from their original small, regional nature to conferences of international character. The success of this transformation, and the recognition that ancient historians needed and were capable of supporting a major professional society, prompted the meeting at Harvard University in May of 1974 where the bylaws and rules of membership were adopted and the formal title Association of Ancient Historians was approved.

Over its lifetime, and that of its forerunner, the AAH has met at 26 different universities in the United States and Canada, and its membership has grown to nearly 800, including most of the ancient historians in these two countries. The AAH is the largest organization in North America that is devoted exclusively to promoting teaching and scholarship in ancient history.

In addition to electing its officers (a president and secretary-treasurer who hold three-year terms) and passing on matters of common interest, the AAH works with individual universities to organize annual meetings that provide an opportunity to present and discuss research in the field. The AAH informs its members through a regular newsletter, sponsors the publication of a series of monographs, has published a volume of collected essays, and has organized summer institutes for college teachers under the sponsorship of the National Endowment for the Humanities. It maintains a home page http://weber.u.washington.edu/~clio/aah/aah.html where several kinds of information are provided including a directory of ancient historians in the U.S., currently under revision, and links to the directory of ancient historians in Canada.

Membership dues are $5.00/year (or $3.00/year for students, retired professors and non-residents of the U.S.). To join, send your name and address along with dues to: Prof. Patricia Dintrone, Department of History, San Diego State University, San Diego, CA 92182.